# Praise for *Four-Dimensional Education*

## From International Organizations

"*Four-Dimensional Education* **provides a rare and profound strategic conversation about education.** By questioning the often-unstated and dated consensus about what young people learn at school, the authors make explicit the systemic boundaries that shape what is learned. Drawing the analytical lines around what is learned can be seen as an invitation to stay within the existing borders or as a challenge to step outside by imagining systemically different goals and organization of learning. *Four-Dimensional Education* encourages both kinds of innovative thinking."

—Riel Miller, Head of Futures,
**UNESCO**

"The content of any nation's curriculum defines its values and reflects its hopes for future generations. In focussing on the 'what' of curriculum design, *Four-Dimensional Education* **provides a rich and practical provocation which can inspire policymakers and practitioners.**"

—Joe Hallgarten, Director of Education, and leader of
*Grand Curriculum Designs*,
**The Royal Society for the Arts (RSA)**

"*Four Dimensional Education* **brings a deeply cogent, synthetic, open-minded conversation to explore** one of the key challenges to our society—**how to transform our education systems to** respond effectively to global 21st century needs and aspirations. USCIB has been privileged to be part of this conversation through a series of sponsored roundtables with the CCR bringing educators together with economists and business to bring new insights and perspectives to help students **build the world we want.**"

—Peter M. Robinson, CEO and President,
**United States Council for International Business (USCIB)**

## From Corporations

"**What should students learn in an age of search, robotics and artificial intelligence?** The acceleration of technology and explosion of information creates the urgent need to rethink an educational system that is traditionally centered on content. Starting with a deep understanding of how modern society and workforce needs are changing, this book challenges us to take a big leap in education curricula to reflect **deep competencies, including relevant modern knowledge.**"

—Steve Vinter, Director, Cambridge site,
**Google**

"**A must read for anyone interested in the future of education** in a rapidly changing world. The best way to predict the future is to inspire the next generation of students to build it better."

—Jim Spohrer, Director of University Programs,
**IBM**

"**This book should be required reading for everyone involved in education and education reform.** Fadel and colleagues have developed a unique language and framework map for enabling diverse stakeholders to find commonalities in their differences as well as a collection of tools to aid in developing and comparing innovative systems."

—John Abele, Founding Chairman of **Boston Scientific**,
Chairman of the **Argosy Foundation**

"**As scientists, humanitarians, engineers, and artists... as lifelong teachers and learners... as parents, and as humans... we owe it to our children to continuously prune our education curriculum, and to feed it with the nutrients of advancement**— in ways which our children will encounter them in their careers, and in their lives. We must contextualize our curricula with explicit interdisciplinary constructs that will teach them how to think, how to learn, how to synthesize information and apply critical discernment. In this "living book," the authors lay an analytical and pragmatic foundation for a novel look at K–12 education goals—one that embraces the whole brain, the whole person, and all of society's needs. ***Four-Dimensional Education poses a healthy challenge to the traditional, less-relevant structures of today's curricula.*** Let this book be a call to action to all of us to join in CCR's mission, and to become actively involved in shaping the future of earth."

—Kristen Wright, Director, Cisco Research & Open Innovation
**Cisco Systems**

**"Education needs fundamental reform from top to bottom. This book puts square and center the need for that change at every level of thinking** from curricula to pedagogy to assessment—laying out a much-needed structure into which the fundamental maths and STEM reforms we are pioneering at computerbasedmath.org can fit."

—Conrad Wolfram, founder,
**Wolfram Research Europe**

## From Academic Institutions

"*Four-Dimensional Education* describes a comprehensive framework for what personalized education for the 21st century must be about: comprehensive and adaptive while allowing for choice and local needs, along all dimensions of an education not merely traditional knowledge. **Educators and policymakers worldwide owe it to students and societies to rapidly operationalize these dimensions of knowledge, skills, character, and meta-learning.**"

—Todd Rose, Director of the Mind, Brain & Education program at the
Graduate School of Education,
**Harvard University**

"*Four-Dimensional Education* charts a lucid course between two research frontiers, one assessing how astounding new technologies are reshaping our future job opportunities and skill demands, and the second striving to equip our future workforce (our kids) with the skills to compete and to thrive in that future. Traversing those two frontiers, **this book offers a wise and practical set of insights for empowering students and citizens to analyze, communicate, interact, and adapt.**"

—David Autor, Professor of Economics and Associate Department Head
**Massachusetts Institute of Technology**

"A very thoughtful treatment of the competencies our students need to thrive in today's (and tomorrow's) world. This book will help educators understand and navigate the critical choices we are facing."

—**Carol Dweck**, Lewis & Virginia Eaton Professor of Psychology,
Department of Psychology,
**Stanford University**

"Arguably the biggest challenge facing the human race in the 21st century is education, yet few organizations have given this as much thought and analysis as the Center for Curriculum Redesign. What does every child need to know in this age? Our system of education hasn't changed significantly in centuries, yet the knowledge, skills, and character needed now are fundamentally changing. I highly recommend this book to anyone who cares about the future. **It is insightful, comprehensive, global, and coherent. It will set the compass direction for the next generation**."

—Rick Miller, President
**Olin College of Engineering**

"Exponential technologies are providing us with extraordinary opportunities for solving the biggest challenges we face, but are also disrupting the old ways of doing things. *Four-Dimensional Education* **establishes a framework for continuous learning that is necessary for youth and adults alike to stay relevant and to thrive in these exponential times.**"

—Rob Nail, Associate Founder & CEO
**Singularity University**

## From Foundations and Non-Profit Organizations

"As communities around the world work to ensure that all children have access to the kind of education that enables them to fulfill their true potential, the first question must be: What are our ultimate aims? The answers to this question will vary based on community context and culture, and yet these answers must be informed by a sense of global responsibility and an understanding of what the world will require of today's children. **This book**—a treasure trove from some of the world's foremost educational leaders—provides the latest understanding about the knowledge, skills, character, and meta-learning that will be required for global success. It **is an incredible resource for local educators around the world who want to put their students on a path toward shaping the future.**"

—Wendy Kopp, CEO and Co-founder,
**Teach For All**

"*Four-Dimensional Education* **offers a compelling vision for transforming education and how we look at education.** In a global economy, driven by nimbleness and innovation, it is increasingly clear that success depends on the transformation of education system. This book challenges us to redefine what we mean by success at all levels of the education system from the foundations of K–12, to the entrance requirements for higher education, to what the workforce can and needs to be."

—Matt Williams Vice President, Policy and Advocacy,
**KnowledgeWorks Foundation**

"*Four-Dimensional Education* provides a compelling, updated view of why education must change across the globe and what it should look like in the future, building on Fadel's and Trilling's first book, *21$^{st}$ Century Skills*. In clear, easy to understand language, they **articulate what 21$^{st}$ century learners need to be successful—a must read for us all.**"

—Dr. Helen Soule, Executive Director of P21,
**The Partnership for 21st Century Learning**

"We applaud CCR's distillation of vast research on the future of education in this accessible and compelling new book. ***Four-Dimensional Education* is a *must read* for every globally minded leader and teacher interested in advancing their institutions through innovation. Similarly, parents interested in relevant 21$^{st}$ century education should read this book as well!**"

—Heather Hoerle, Executive Director,
**Secondary School Admission Test Board**

"Reading *Four-Dimensional Education* and its focus on making education more relevant in a world which is changing exponentially, reminded me of Harold Benjamin's timeless satire,

'The Saber Tooth Curriculum' written in 1939. It tells of a fictional prehistoric society where "Saber Tooth Tiger Scaring" with fire is still part of the curriculum, though said tiger is extinct. Fast forward to the 21st century and the accelerating pace of change driven in large measure by the learners of the 20th century who somehow learned to be adaptable, savvy, versatile, collaborative and empathetic—sometimes within formal learning frameworks, often outside. In short they made the curriculum extinct. Instead of being saber-toothed they were laser-focused. **By drafting a dynamic framework for learning that adapts to and reflects success,** *Four-Dimensional Education* **will serve as a catalyst for lifelong learning and reinvention. The quality of our generational futures hinges on success."**

—David F. Clune Ph. D, President and CEO<br>
**Educational Records Bureau (ERB)**

"Our current circumstances cry out for a new model of education. **This book** provides one and **will be a powerful tool in the hands of those committed to preparing their students for the challenges of 21st century life and work."**

—Ken Kay and Valerie Greenhill, co-founders of EdLeader21<br>
and co-authors of *The Leader's Guide to 21st Century Education: 7 Steps<br>
for Schools and Districts*

# FOUR-DIMENSIONAL EDUCATION

Charles Fadel, Maya Bialik, and Bernie Trilling

The Center for Curriculum Redesign, Boston, MA, 02130

Copyright © 2015 by Center for Curriculum Redesign

All rights reserved. Published 2015.

Printed in the United States of America

*Four-Dimensional Education: The Competencies Learners Need to Succeed*

ISBN-13: 978-1518642562

ISBN-10: 151864256X

Keywords: Curriculum, Standards, Competencies, Competency, CBL, Deeper Learning, Knowledge, Skills, Character, Metacognition, Meta-Learning, 21st Century Education, Education Technology, EdTech, Social-Emotional Skills, 21st Century Competencies, Education Redesign, 21st Century Curriculum, Pedagogy, Learning, Jobs, Employment, Employability, Eduployment, Education 2030, Mindset.

With sincere gratitude to all external sources; their contribution is used for nonprofit education work under the fair use doctrine of copyright laws.

# Dedications and Thanks

**From Charles:**

To the countless people yearning for a fulfilling life—you are my inner motivation, thank you!

To (alphabetically) Aline, Carole, and Nathalie, for their love, and with all of mine.

To (alphabetically) John Abele, Randa Grob-Zakhary, Henri Moser, and Attilio Oliva for their trust and caring guidance.

To my wonderful co-authors, for their significant patience and numerous expert contributions.

And for a sustainable humanity through empowered learners!


**From Maya:**

To the hundreds of millions of students spending a significant proportion of their childhoods in formal education systems around the world—may this work help to improve this experience.

To my father, who worked his whole life to provide me with the best possible education opportunities, complemented them with countless hours of patient one-on-one teaching, made every moment an opportunity for learning, and supported my decisions as long as I was pushing myself to grow and improve.

And to my sister—my first educational experiment subject, my younger twin. You're awesome.


**From Bernie:**

To the joy of learning, and to all who inspire small sparks to bloom into lifelong adventures—thank you for helping dreams really happen, and for the world to be a little happier place for us all.

The authors wish to thank all of the following for their insights, ideas and contributions to this writing and to CCR's work (alphabetically by last name):

John Abele, Peter Bishop, Michele Bruniges, Jennifer Chidsey, Jillian Darwish, Keri Facer, Devin Fidler, Kurt Fisher, Jennifer Groff, Ellen Hambrook, Dan Hoffman, Michaela Horvathova, Myra LalDin, Christine Lee, SaeYun Lee, Doug Lynch, Tony Mackay, Riel Miller, Rick Miller, Marco Morales, Peter Nilsson, Melissa Panchuck, Ignacio Peña, Robert Plotkin, Didier Raboud, Todd Rose, Courtney Ross, Andreas Schleicher, Dirk Van Damme, Erja Vitikka, Jim Wynn and many others—in particular all the reviewers in the "Praise" section, and the Education 2030 team at OECD.

# Table of Contents

**Chapter Eight**

# Prologue

# Why Rethinking the *What* of Education Matters So Much

By Andreas Schleicher, Director for Education and Skills, Organization for Economic Co-operation and Development (OECD)

The demands on learners and thus education systems are evolving fast. In the past, education was about teaching people something. Now, it's about making sure that individuals develop a reliable compass and the navigation skills to find their own way through an increasingly uncertain, volatile, and ambiguous world. These days, we no longer know exactly how things will unfold. Often we are surprised and need to learn from the extraordinary, and sometimes we make mistakes along the way. And it will often be the mistakes and failures, when properly understood, that create the context for learning and growth. A generation ago, teachers could expect that what they taught would last for a lifetime for their students. Today, schools need to prepare students for more rapid economic and social change than ever before, for jobs that have not yet been created, to use technologies that have not yet been invented, and to solve social problems that we don't yet know will arise.

How do we foster motivated, engaged learners who are prepared to conquer the unforeseen challenges of tomorrow, not to speak of those of today? The dilemma for educators is that the skills that are easiest to teach and easiest to test, are also the skills that are easiest to digitize, automate, and outsource. There is no question that state-of-the-art knowledge in a discipline will always remain important. Innovative or creative people generally have specialized skills in a field of knowledge or a practice. And as much as skills of learning to learn are important, we always learn by learning something. Educational success is no longer mainly about reproducing content knowledge, but about extrapolating from what we know and applying that knowledge in novel situations. Put simply, the world no longer rewards people just for what they know—search engines know everything—but for what they can do with what they know, how they behave in the world, and how they adapt. Because that is the main differentiator today, education is becoming more about creativity, critical thinking, communication, and collaboration; about modern knowledge, including the capacity to recognize and exploit the potential of new technologies; and, last but not least, about the character qualities that help fulfilled people live and work together and build a sustainable humanity.

Conventionally our approach to problems was breaking them down into manageable bits and pieces, and then to teach students the techniques to solve them. But today we also create value by synthesizing the disparate bits. This is about curiosity, open-mindedness, and making connections between ideas that previously seemed unrelated, which requires being familiar with and receptive to knowledge in other fields than our own. If we spend our whole life in a silo of a single discipline, we will not gain the imaginative skills to connect the dots where the next invention will come from.

The world is also no longer divided into specialists and generalists. Specialists have deep skills and narrow scope, giving them expertise that is recognized by peers but not valued outside their domain. Generalists have broad scope but shallow skills. What counts increasingly are the *versatilists* who are able to apply depth of skill to a progressively widening scope of situations and experiences, gaining new competencies, building relationships, and assuming new roles. They are capable of constantly adapting and also of constantly learning and growing, of positioning themselves and repositioning themselves in a fast-changing world.

Perhaps most importantly, in today's schools, students typically learn individually and, at the end of the school year, we certify their individual achievements. But the more interdependent the world becomes, the more we rely on great collaborators and orchestrators who are able to join others in life, work, and citizenship. Innovation, too, is now rarely the product of individuals working in isolation but an outcome of how we mobilize, share, and link knowledge. So schools need to prepare students for a world in which many people need to collaborate with people of diverse cultural origins, and appreciate different ideas, perspectives, and values; a world in which people need to decide how to trust and collaborate across such differences; and a world in which their lives will be affected by issues that transcend national boundaries. Expressed differently, schools need to drive a shift from a world where traditional knowledge is depreciating rapidly in value, towards a world in which the enriching power of deep competencies is increasing, based on a relevant blend of traditional and modern knowledge, along with skills, character qualities, and self-directed learning.

In many schools around the world, teachers and school leaders are working hard to help learners develop these kinds of knowledge, skills, and character competencies. But the status quo has many protectors, as anyone who has tried to make room in today's crowded school curricula for new educational content will know. The results have been the kind of mile-wide but inch-deep, overloaded yet only partially relevant curricula that dominate today's classrooms, and that severely constrain the development of deep competencies and the use of advanced pedagogy.

The foundational reason for why we find it so difficult to rebuild school curricula around the needs of the modern world is that we lack an organizing framework that can help prioritize educational competencies, and systematically structure the conversation around what individuals should learn at various stages of their development. **Four-Dimensional Education provides a clear and actionable, first-of-its-kind organizing framework of competencies needed for this century. Its main innovation lies in not presenting yet another one-size-fits-all list of what individuals should learn, but in crisply defining the spaces in which educators, curriculum planners, policymakers and learners can establish what should be learned, in their context and for their future.** The OECD's Education 2030 project will collaboratively build on this foundational work by

CCR, and the OECD is currently developing a competencies framework by conducting an in-depth international comparative curriculum framework analysis. Drawing on the OECD's global convening power, the framework will be tested, refined, and validated in an interactive manner with multilevel stakeholders in the global community.

# Introduction

> We cannot solve our problems with the same
> thinking we used when we created them.
> —Albert Einstein

Education—which refers to formal schooling in this book—is a fundamental part of the development of every citizen of every country on earth. It is meant to prepare students to thrive in the world, and has the potential to be a powerful tool for social progress. If designed well, education can lead to more empowered and happier individuals, more peaceful, sustainable societies, with more economic progress and fairness, composed of people who are fulfilled across all the dimensions of their well-being.

How are we doing, globally, at achieving these lofty goals of education?

It's difficult to measure directly, but there are a few hints. Economic inequality is growing, education is misaligned with employment opportunities, and violence continues around the globe. To make matters worse, the world is changing at an increasing pace. We are now witnessing transformations—dramatic, wide-sweeping changes such as international mobility, shifts in family structures, increasing diversity in populations, globalization and its impacts on economic competitiveness and social cohesion, new and emerging occupations and careers, rapid and continued advances in technology and its increased use, and so on. And technological changes are happening at an exponential rate, often exacerbating existing societal challenges. In other words, the world that our education was designed for no longer exists, and even if we redesign an education system for the world as it is right now, it will be partially outdated by the time the current first graders graduate high school. So what can we do? We must redesign the curriculum with this unavoidable state of change in mind, and train students to be adaptable and versatile.

This is an opportunity. Humanity can reflect, adapt, and act proactively to shape the future we want. Many educational programs focus on improving *how* education is implemented. This is a worthy and important goal. But here we ask, are we teaching and testing the right things? *What* should be learned to best prepare our students for the twenty-first century?

In this book, the Center for Curriculum Redesign (CCR) explores a framework built to address this question, so curriculum can catch up to our current world and be positioned for the uncertain future. The framework focuses on knowledge (what students know and understand), skills (how they use that knowledge), character (how they behave and engage in the world), and meta-learning (how they reflect on themselves and adapt by continuing to learn and grow toward their goals).

This book is for teachers, department heads, heads of schools, administrators, policymakers, standard setters, curriculum and assessment developers, and other thought leaders and influencers, who seek to develop a thorough understanding of the needs and challenges we all face, and to help devise innovative solutions.

## A Special Note to Our Readers

This book is a living, adaptive document. It will evolve as we learn more about effective education and as the world continues to change.

To reflect this evolution and to serve our readers, we are using a software model in the distribution of the e-book version. Each registered purchaser will be entitled to a 50 percent reduction in the price of following revisions, which will be published when significant updates to the framework are made.

To register for your ebook update discount, please visit:

http://curriculumredesign.org

# Chapter 1

# Redesigning Education for a Transforming World

The future ain't what it used to be.

—Yogi Berra

## Global Trends and Challenges

What can we as individuals, and collectively as a society, do to ensure that we have a positive effect on the world? The goals for a better future can widely be agreed upon: more peaceful, sustainable societies, comprised of more personally fulfilled people, making full use of their potential. These same goals can be thought of in a number of ways—high levels of civic and social engagement, personal health and well-being, employment in good quality jobs, economic productivity, ecological sustainability, and so on.

Educating our children, in theory, is meant to prepare them to fit in with the world of the future, empowering them to actively work to improve it further. Yet there is growing evidence (as we will see later) from scientific studies, from employer surveys, from widespread public opinion, and from educators themselves, that our education systems, globally, are not delivering fully on this promise—students are often not adequately prepared to succeed in today's, let alone tomorrow's, world.

One reason is that the world continues to transform dramatically, while education is not adapting quickly enough to meet all the demands these transformations are bringing. The challenges and opportunities of today are starkly different from those of the Industrial Revolution, when the first blueprint for a then-modern education system was crafted. They are even different from the challenges of just a couple of decades ago, before the Internet. The world's new, electronic hyper-connectedness poses an entirely new breed and scale of potential problems.

We can see these new problems in recent events such as the 2008 global economic recession. In the past, when a small number of banks in one country may have had difficulties, each had to suffer the consequences alone; now, when one part of a system fails, the negative consequences propagate throughout our interwoven economic systems, causing major problems worldwide. Our social systems, now connected into vast, global communication ecosystems, are more vulnerable to widespread global disruptions; they have grown large and fragile.[1] On top of that, we are struggling to reconcile our hopes and expectations of economic growth with overpopulation, overconsumption, and their consequences on our climate and resources.

The World Economic Forum recently brought together experts in economics, geopolitics, sociology, technology, and environmental sciences, and from business, academia, NGOs, and governments, to compile a list of the most pressing world trends and challenges. They graphed the interconnections between these various trends, highlighting important connections, such as the links between rising income disparity and dramatic increases in the risks from social instability, as shown in Figure 1.1.[2]

---

[1] N. N. Taleb, *Antifragile: Things That Gain from Disorder* (New York: Random House 2012).
[2] More on their methods here: http://reports.weforum.org/global-risks-2015/appendix-b-the-global-risks-perception-survey-2014-and-methodology/

**Figure 1.1 Global Trends and Risks**
*Source:* World Education Forum

Note: This graphic highlights the interaction of global trends (grey pentagons),[3] and risks (colored diamonds—economic risks are blue, environmental risks green, geopolitical risks orange, societal risks red, and technological risks purple). The size of each diamond node corresponds to the degree of impact and likelihood of that risk.

These trends and risks are not ones we could have predicted 50 years ago, and they will continue to interact and evolve in unexpected and unpredictable ways. Meanwhile students continue to study the same curriculum, not prepared to face the challenges in our world.

---

[3] If you have black and white print version, please refer to the website.

# Sustainability

The magnitude of the change of scale in human impacts is a relatively new development. Our global human population has, historically speaking, only recently exploded to an unsustainable rate.[4]

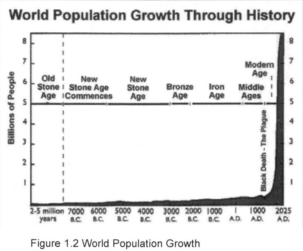

Figure 1.2 World Population Growth
*Source:* Population Reference Bureau

Since we are all in a globally interconnected and interdependent network of life-support systems, this population explosion has large consequences. Our societies are caught up in a web of consumption and competition patterns, and we are rapidly using up the resources we rely on to survive.

Globally, the average resources we now use in one year take the earth about 1.5 years to produce.[5] Depending on a country's lifestyle and degree of consumption, the land needed to support its level of resource use can translate into the number of earths we would need to support all of humanity, if everyone on

---

[4] Elaine M. Murphy, *World Population: Toward the Next Century* (Washington, DC, Population Reference Bureau, 1994).
[5] Global Footprint Network,
www.footprintnetwork.org/en/index.php/GFN/page/world_footprint

the planet consumed resources at the rate of that one country (as seen in Figure 1.3).[6]

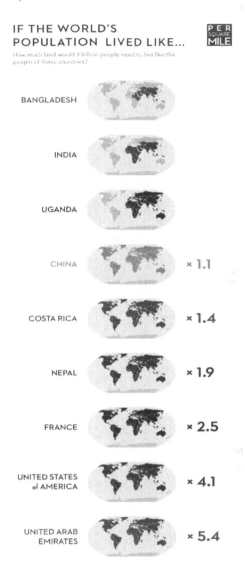

IF THE WORLD'S
POPULATION LIVED LIKE...

PER
SQUARE
MILE

How much land would 7 billion people need to live like the people of those countries?

BANGLADESH

INDIA

UGANDA

CHINA          × 1.1

COSTA RICA     × 1.4

NEPAL          × 1.9

FRANCE         × 2.5

UNITED STATES
of AMERICA     × 4.1

UNITED ARAB
EMIRATES       × 5.4

Figure 1.3 Populations and Land
*Source:* Global Footprint Network, http://www.footprintnetwork.org

---

[6] Christine McDonald, "How Many Earths Do We Need?" BBC News, www.bbc.com/news/magazine-33133712

According to a number of scientists, we have already effected environmental changes that could cause our extinction. There are many historic examples of similar collective human dead-end actions operating on smaller scales. The tribes of Easter Island competed with each other so fiercely (including the competitive creation of the iconic massive statues) that they used up all the available resources on the island, and their civilization collapsed.

According to evolutionary biologist Jared Diamond, the parallels between the downfall of civilization on Easter Island and today's world are "chillingly obvious." In his book, *Collapse*, he follows the arcs of several civilizations that have vanished, and shows the similarities between them and our global civilization today. Diamond writes:

> Because we are rapidly advancing along this non-sustainable course, the world's environmental problems will get resolved, in one way or another, within the lifetimes of the children and young adults alive today. The only question is whether they will become resolved in pleasant ways of our own choice, or in unpleasant ways not of our choice, such as warfare, genocide, starvation, disease epidemics, and collapses of societies.[7]

The survival of the human race depends on our ability to put our knowledge into action across disciplines and political divides. Education can be a powerful tool for survival, but the competencies to meet these challenges are currently not being taught consistently and effectively.

---

[7] Jared Diamond, *Collapse: How Societies Choose to Fail or Succeed* (Penguin: New York, 2005), 498.

# VUCA and Values

An acronym has emerged to describe a future that will consist of greater volatility, uncertainty, complexity, and ambiguity: VUCA. The use of the acronym VUCA began in the late 1990s in a military context. It has subsequently influenced emerging ideas on strategic leadership in a wide range of organizations, from for-profit corporations to educational institutions and governmental systems. Generally, it warns that our world is becoming increasingly difficult to predict and manage.

Our future depends, in part, on our values. Consumerism and materialism trends, while unsustainable in the long term, are to a large extent socially and culturally determined, and therefore can change as a culture's values shift. Societal values also determine where a particular culture lies on various values continua such as antagonism and tolerance, individualism and social cohesion, and materialism and the search for deeper meaning. As we begin to collectively consider alternative values that would be more globally sustainable and personally fulfilling, we are responding to both pushes, based on necessity and anxiety about the direction our current values are taking us, and pulls from the desire for better societal systems based on altered values (see Table 1.1).

| Pushes | Pulls |
|---|---|
| Anxiety about the future | Promise of security and social cohesion |
| Concern that policy adjustments are insufficient to avoid crises | Ethics of taking personal responsibility for others, nature, and the future |
| Fear of loss of freedom and choice | Engaged participation in community, political and cultural life |
| Alienation from dominant culture | Pursuit of personal meaning and purpose |
| Stressful lifestyles | Time for personal passions and stronger connections to nature |

Table 1.1 Pushes and Pulls
*Source:* P. Raskin et.al., *The Great Transition: The Promise and Lure of Times Ahead* (Boston, MA: Stockholm Environment Institute, 2002).

The value systems that arise from these pushes and pulls can embrace both aspirational and inspirational goals, rather than merely adopting defensive or depressive attitudes. Being aware of the powerful forces that contribute to our modern life, we can act as agents with intention and a design mindset, and not just impulsively react to the dramatic changes around us. This agency, necessary to change the world, needs to be reflected in an effective twenty-first century education.

# Exponential Progress and Future Predictions

> It's difficult to make predictions, especially about the future.
>
> —Mark Twain

For the human mind, accustomed to thinking linearly, exponential change is a difficult concept to grasp. Consider the Indian legend in which a local king challenges the god Krishna to a chess game. They decide to bet one grain of rice on the first square, and double the amount on each square thereafter. Having lost the game, the king begins to arrange the rice according to their agreement, but soon realizes he would not be able to fulfill his promise. One grain of rice is not much, and doubling doesn't seem like much either, but the growth is exponential. By the twentieth square, the King would have had to put down 1 million grains of rice, and 2 million on the next. By the last square, it would be more than one hundred quadrillion grains of rice—equivalent to more than 1000 times the current world rice production.

Computing and communication technologies grow in a similar way. For transistors in circuits there is even a special name for the observation that progress happens exponentially: Moore's Law. Moore's Law states that the density of transistors doubles every 1.5 to 2 years, with corresponding increases in computational speed and storage capacity.

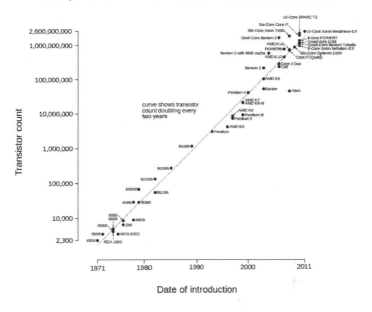

**Figure 1.4 Moore's Law**
*Source:* Wikimedia Commons,
https://commons.wikimedia.org/wiki/File:Transistor_Count_and_Moore
%27s_Law_-
_2011.svg#/media/File:Transistor_Count_and_Moore%27s_Law_-
_2011.svg.

Thus today we are experiencing a massive revolution in communication in the form of the Internet. It is the first truly global, interactive, social, communication medium that is accessible to a significant number of the world's population. Ideas, images, and sounds zip around the world at the speed of light, disrupting industries and cultures along the way. Put another way, to reach an audience of 50 million people it took radio 38 years, television 13 years, the Internet four years, and Facebook only two years. The speed of technological change today is vastly greater than it was even several years ago—innovations in technology are being adopted at exponential rates, vastly more rapid than in any prior time in civilization.

Typically, we make predictions about the future by extrapolating from the past, but this can often lead us astray. In

2004, the best-selling mobile phone was the Nokia 2600, a single-function cellular telephone. Phones were expected to get smaller and smaller, with no other significant changes. Yet only three years later, the first iPhone was introduced, and it altered the course of the design and use of mobile phones, which became smartphones. Now our "phones" are significantly larger than the old Nokia, have almost no buttons, and exist in an ecosystem of apps that relate to every aspect of life.

This would have been very difficult to predict from the trends in 2004, because the change was discontinuous with the trends. Similarly, any predictions we make now about education are bound to be partially wrong. We cannot depend on current predictions based on recent trends to carve our future educational goals, standards, and curricula in stone. Rather, we must create flexible guidelines that help prepare our students to be versatile enough to succeed no matter how our unpredictable world changes around us.

A succinct representation of versatility, transcending an employer's perspective, can be visualized via IBM's *T*-shaped individual[8]—one who is capable of both depth *and* breadth.

**Breadth of Knowledge**

Figure 1.5 T-Shaped Individual
*Source:* Jim Spohrer, IBM

------

[8]Jim Spohrer, *Slideshare*, www.slideshare.net/spohrer/t-shaped-people-20130628-v5

It is expected that over the life of an individual, several types of expertise will be developed—an *M*-shaped individual. Although it is extremely difficult to predict with any specificity the important technological breakthroughs of the distant future, various organizations have made well-informed attempts at predicting large-scale patterns of the near future. A comparison of three of these, showing how they align across general categories or themes, is shown in Table 1.2.

| KnowledgeWorks Foundation (Forecast 2020)[9] | World Future Society (Top 10 breakthroughs of the next 20–30 years) | McKinsey Global Institute (Top 12 economically disruptive technologies)[10] |
|---|---|---|
| Human Lifespan Increase | — | Next Generation Genomics |
| Connected People, Organizations & Planet | Global Internet access<br><br>Virtual Education | Mobile Internet |
| Rise of Smart Machines & Systems | Quantum Computers Nanotechnology<br><br>Smart Robots | Automation of Knowledge and Work<br><br>Advanced Robotics<br><br>Autonomous and Near-autonomous Vehicles<br><br>3D Printing of Parts<br><br>Advanced Materials |
| Massive Data & New Media | Entertainment on Demand | Internet of Things<br><br>Cloud Technology |
| Environmental Stresses & Demands | Alternative Energy<br><br>Desalination of Water<br><br>Precision Farming | Energy Storage<br><br>Advanced Oil and Gas Exploration Renewable Energy |
| Amplified Humans | Biometrics | — |

Table 1.2 Trend Comparisons
*Source:* CCR

---

[9] KnowledgeWorks Foundation, Forecast 2020, as discussed in the Exponential Progress section of this chapter.
[10] James Manyika et al., *Disruptive Technologies: Advances That Will Transform Life, Business, and the Global Economy,* McKinsey Global Institute (May 2013),
www.mckinsey.com/insights/business_technology/disruptive_technologies

These trends will likely have profound implications for both the relevant content students will need to learn, and the innovative ways they will be learning it in twenty-first century education systems (more on this in Chapter 3, "The Knowledge Dimension").

# Technology's Impact on Society

> Technology gives us power, but it does not, and cannot, tell us how to use that power.
> —Jonathan Sacks

We have been apprehensive of technology changing society for a very long time. Socrates famously believed that writing would "create forgetfulness in the learners' souls" and thus did not record his own words and work. In a way, he was right.

Compare our memorization ability with those of people with long-standing oral traditions who could recite epic works such as the *Iliad* entirely from memory—and our modern culture seems incredibly memory deficient. For the majority of humanity's history, it was commonplace to hold entire books in one's mind, a skill that has become obsolete, and thus, no longer practiced. If Socrates time traveled to today's world, he would be appalled at how little we memorize, and how much we rely on memory aids outside of our own minds.

And yet, writing things down has given us a collective history that can be viewed and added to at any time, allowing people to build on and critique each other's work. So this concern about technology's impact is at once a very old worry about very real consequences, and a source of great hope, as technology has the potential to be empowering and world-changing.

Critics of technology's impact on society point to increasing rates of childhood obesity, face-to-face socializing being replaced by multi-user video games, addictive and withdrawal-like behaviors from excessive media use, and lower comprehension when reading from electronic sources versus paper ones. Yet many of these aspects are being addressed by new technology adaptations and new ways of using existing technologies. Games are now being intentionally developed to include face-to-face collaboration and interactions in the real world. The aspects of games that make them addictive (autonomy, mastery, and purpose) are being better understood and harnessed for more powerful learning experiences.[11] The nuances of comprehension differences in reading from differing media types are being further explored, and may be addressed by future technology innovations.

Every breakthrough has this potential for both positive and negative effects—progress is truly a double-edged sword, and technology is an amoral amplifier. For instance, the commercialization and commoditization of knowledge on the Internet can lead to much wider access to knowledge, instant distribution, and sharing of ideas. But it can also lead to the spread of more dangerous knowledge such as 3D-printed weapons, home-grown biological warfare agents, and so on. Scientific discoveries are subject to the same duality—nuclear energy can be used as a positive, abundant energy source, or it can be used to make powerfully negative, destructive weapons.

An important point to underscore here is that we may not be able to stop the accelerating progress of invention and technology, but we can carefully manage how they are used in our lives. We need to be very explicit in what we most want out of technology, so that its negative effects will continue to be curbed and its positive potentials continue to be enhanced. We need to be highly intentional about using technology as an empowering tool for reaching our goals, not just for its appeal as a novelty or crutch.

Our education systems need to focus on the universally positive goals of building personal competencies, expertise, and wisdom for all learners. All students need to learn to consider the wider implications of their actions, to act mindfully in the world, and to reflect and adapt as the world changes.

---

[11]   D. H. Pink, *Drive: The Surprising Truth About What Motivates Us* (New York: Penguin, 2011).

# Technology, Automation, Outsourcing and Jobs

> We are currently preparing students for jobs that don't yet exist, using technologies that haven't been invented, in order to solve problems we don't even know are problems yet.
>
> —Richard Riley

Technology first removed much of the dirt, sweat, and dangers from physical work. Then it took away many of the dull mental tasks that could be automated, and now it threatens to even displace some tasks that require expert decision-making.[12] As an example, computers are being trained to diagnose breast cancer, with the potential for including many more factors than human doctors are able to consider in a given instant.[13]

But does this mean that humans will necessarily be squeezed out of all of their occupations? As computers are beginning to drive cars and take restaurant orders, this thought is floating to the surface of the public discussion. Or could it mean that more people will be freed up to do more meaningful work, and use more powerful tools to their advantage in their tasks? Could more people follow their passions more deeply, and have more of a positive influence on the world?

Human work and expertise comes in many different forms and flavors. Based on the variety of shifts in technology used in different countries around the world, some jobs are now being automated or performed at lower costs in other countries, and the exact needs for certain types of jobs in particular locations are

---

[12] For an in-depth treatment of the subject, see Erik Brynjolfsson, *The Second Machine Age: Work, Progress, and Prosperity in a Time of Brilliant Technologies* (New York: W. W. Norton, 2014).

[13] Andrew Beck et al.,"Systematic Analysis of Breast Cancer Morphology Uncovers Stromal Features Associated with Survival," *Science Translational Medicine* 3 (2011), http://med.stanford.edu/labs/vanderijn-west/documents/108ra113.full.pdf

disappearing and reappearing in very high demand somewhere else in the world.

Figures 1.6 and 1.7 are representations of how job types have changed since 1850 in both percentages and real numbers.

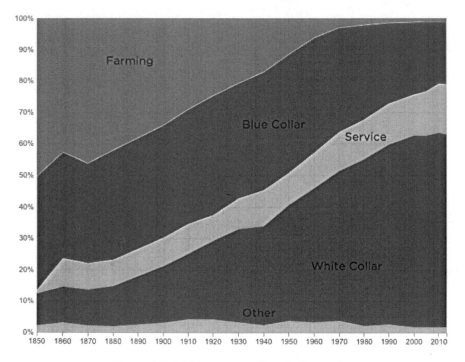

Figure 1.6 Job Types over Time in Percentages
Source: IPUMS-USA, University of Minnesota

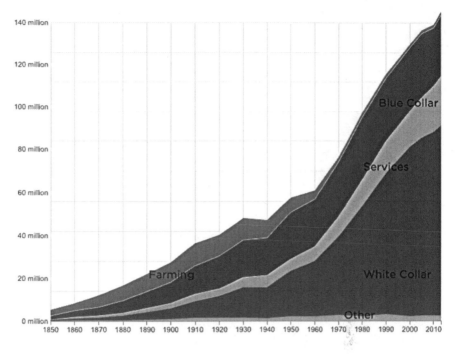

Figure 1.7 Job Types over Time in Numbers
*Source:* IPUMS-USA, University of Minnesota

The intuitive notion that technological progress would make jobs easier and create more leisure time is proving to be untrue. People are working just as much, if not longer and harder, and producing more and more. Even as certain types of jobs become automated, entirely new kinds of jobs appear, such as social media manager, and cloud services engineer.

Automation is not a new phenomenon. Horses were replaced by cars, medieval scribes by the Gutenberg printing press, and launderers by washing machines, cashiers by checkout barcode scanners, credit card readers, mobile phone payment chips, and so on. And recently, retailer H&M has admitted to using mannequins' bodies "with no flaws" in place of human models.

Figure 1.8 Mannequins—Only the Faces Are Real
*Source: Le Monde Culture and Ideas,*
December 24, 2011

This leads us to important questions:

• What types of occupations are subject to automation and what types are not?

• More precisely, to what degree?

• What new jobs get created, and what competencies will they require?

• How do we prepare our students for the jobs that will actually exist when they graduate?

First, we must understand how automation works. Generally speaking, computers can execute a program that follows a pattern, or a set of rules. Their strengths are speed and accuracy, whereas humans' strengths are flexibility and synthesis. Figure 1.9 shows some examples, ranging from easy to difficult in terms of programming.

Increasingly Difficult to Program

|  | Rules-Based Logic | Pattern Recognition | Human Work |
|---|---|---|---|
| **Variety** | Computer Processing using Deductive Rules | Computer Processing using Inductive Rules | Rules cannot be Articulated and/or Necessary Information cannot be Obtained |
| **Examples** | Calculate Basic Income Taxes<br><br>Issuing a Boarding Pass | Speech Recognition<br><br>Predicting a Mortgage Default | Writing a Convincing Legal Brief<br><br>Moving Furniture into a Third Floor Apartment |

Figure 1.9 Programming Difficulties
*Source:* Third Way,
http://content.thirdway.org/publications/714/Dancing-With-Robots.pdf

We can see the effect of automation when we examine what types of jobs in the United States have increased and what types have decreased since 1960, as shown in Figure 1.10.

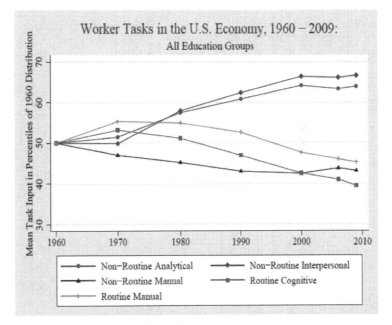

Figure 1.10 Worker Tasks
*Source:* D. Autor, "The Changing Task Composition of the US Labor Market: An Update of Autor, Levy, and Murnane (2003)," MIT (2013), pdf: http://economics.mit.edu/files/9758

Routine tasks, whether manual (e.g., assembly work) or cognitive (e.g., paperwork), can increasingly be automated and thus the demand for the associated skills is dropping. Non-routine manual jobs, such as plumbing, are also declining, but they can only decline so much, as we all continue to need plumbing repairs in our homes. However, with augmented reality, this may again be called into question, as a plumber residing across the world can guide a homeowner's hand (or haptic glove!).

What skills should we be teaching then? *Non-routine, interpersonal skills* (such as those involved in consulting) and *non-routine analytical skills* (such as those in engineering design and medical surgery)—these are the kinds of skills that will be needed in the future.[14]

But there is another layer of detail here. Many skills can also be performed remotely, and as the world becomes increasingly connected, it also becomes increasingly small. If these skills can be provided remotely at a lower cost with the same quality, the local demand for them may decrease. Broadly speaking, tasks that can be completed over a large distance, impersonally, and delivered to the user electronically are easier to offshore.[15]

Combining these two insights, we begin to see a picture of the future emerging. Two main forces determine what jobs will be needed in the future—whether the main tasks require personal delivery (this limits offshore possibilities) or if the tasks are non-routine (this limits automation). Figure 1.11 is a representation of these forces and how different types of jobs are affected.

---

[14]  David Autor and Brendan Price, "The Changing Task Composition of the US Labor Market: An Update of Autor, Levy, and Murnane (2003)," June 21, 2013, pdf: http://economics.mit.edu/files/9758

[15]  Alan S. Blinder, "How Many U.S. Jobs Might Be Offshorable?" Princeton University CEPS Working Paper No. 142, March 2007.

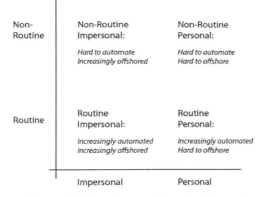

|  | Impersonal | Personal |
|---|---|---|
| Non-Routine | Non-Routine Impersonal:<br><br>*Hard to automate*<br>*Increasingly offshored* | Non-Routine Personal:<br><br>*Hard to automate*<br>*Hard to offshore* |
| Routine | Routine Impersonal:<br><br>*Increasingly automated*<br>*Increasingly offshored* | Routine Personal:<br><br>*Increasingly automated*<br>*Hard to offshore* |

Figure 1.11 Routine and Non-Routine Jobs
*Source:* CCR (using Blinder for X-axis; Autor, Levy, & Murnane for the Y-axis).

As a general rule, this means education for employment needs to refocus away from routinized, impersonal tasks, and toward more complex, personal, creative tasks that only humans can do well. In this way, while there will be a growing need for programmers and other science and technology specialists as technology progresses, it turns out that there will also be a growing need for people who excel at creative and interpersonal tasks. These are the tasks most difficult to automate or offshore, so as computers successfully take over routine tasks, humans are left with the jobs they do best, often using computers as assistive tools to take their products to new heights, instead of being replaced by them.

This general rule may itself change as we learn how to program computers that can process huge amounts of data and make complex cognitive decisions efficiently, creating innovative designs by themselves.[16] The jobs of the future will continue to change, and we must be intentional in order to teach the competencies that continue to be relevant in the world of the future, as well as to students' fulfillment in such a world (more on this in Chapter 3, "The Knowledge Dimension").

---

[16] Such as music! See http://artsites.ucsc.edu/faculty/cope/experiments.htm

# The Race Between Technology and Education

> Civilization is a race between education and catastrophe.
>
> —H. G. Wells

As technology progresses, the education necessary to utilize it effectively also grows, and education must adapt to keep up. In this way, technology and education are in a race.[17]

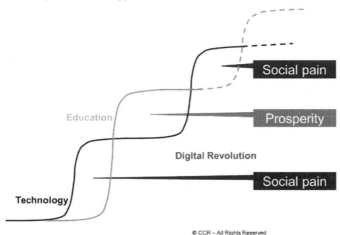

Figure 1.12 Technology and Education
*Source:* CCR (inspired by *The Race between Technology and Education.*)

When education lags behind technological progress, people are not qualified for jobs and the work that does get done is likely not as productive or as high quality as it could be. Additionally, economic inequality grows, as those with the means to get an exceptional education are able to secure more opportunities for advancement, and those without the ability to afford a highly effective education have very little hope of improving their economic status. In this way, both individuals and society suffer in

---

[17] C. D. Goldin and L. F Katz, *The Race between Education and Technology* (Cambridge, MA: Harvard University Press, 2009).

the form of unemployment, underemployment, income gaps, personal stress, and social unrest.

How satisfied are employers and students with the present performance of the education system? According to a study by global consultancy McKinsey, there is a large disconnect (a factor of 2!) between the (mostly satisfied) perception of education providers, and the (mostly dissatisfied) opinion of their customers: the youth themselves and their employers (see Figure 1.13).[18]

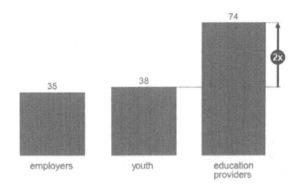

Figure 1.13. Percentage of Respondents Who Agree that Graduates/New Hires Are Adequately Prepared.
Source: "Education to Employment: Getting Europe's Youth into Work," McKinsey & Company, January 2014, www.mckinsey.com/insights/social_sector/converting_education_to_employment _in_europe.

So what should students learn for a world where most of the routinized and impersonal tasks are taken care of by computer systems? Is memorization of large amounts of content still needed in an age where we can find the answer to any question we may have on the Internet?

---

[18] The following are the statements that respondents were asked to agree or disagree with. For employers, "Overall, the entry-level employees we hired in the past year have been adequately prepared by their prehire education and/or training." For youth, "Overall, I think I was adequately prepared for an entry-level position in my chosen career field." For education providers, "Overall, graduates from my institution are adequately prepared for entry-level positions in their chosen field of study."

There are many reasonable answers to these questions, but they rarely focus just on teaching *more* knowledge, rather on learning more relevant knowledge, how to apply that knowledge in new and different ways, and on developing the other three dimensions of learning: skills, character qualities, and meta-learning strategies.

# Chapter 2

# Education Goals for the Twenty-First Century

## The Nature and Evolution of Education Goals

The developmental goals for an individual are succinctly summarized by psychologist Abraham Maslow, called Maslow's Pyramid of Needs (see Figure 2.1).

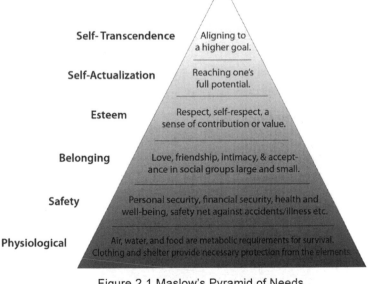

Figure 2.1 Maslow's Pyramid of Needs
*Source:* CCR

The shape of the pyramid highlights the idea that the lower levels are more fundamental to one's well-being, and if those are not fulfilled, the higher level needs will likely not be easily met.

However, this does not mean that they are sequential. All of the levels of need are always present, are important developmental requirements, and can be fulfilled together at the same time.

At the lowest level are one's physiological needs, without which we as biological organisms will cease to function: air, water, food, and shelter from the elements. Just above that are safety and security needs, such as personal security, financial security, health, and safety. An individual who feels that these low-level needs are not being fulfilled, or are uncertain in their lives, cannot easily focus on higher-level goals. This is often the case for students living in poverty, who worry about having enough food, economic security, or have to cope with family stress or violence, and as a result have greater difficulty focusing on the demands of school and its higher need levels.

The next level in Maslow's pyramid focuses on love and belonging. As social animals, it is crucial for people to feel a sense of belonging, to have supportive friendships, a positive family dynamic, and mature, intimate relationships. Just above that is the need for esteem: to feel respected and valued by others, and to feel that one's contributions are important. If these needs are not met, an individual may experience various psychological stresses such as low self-esteem, a lack of confidence and feelings of inferiority. Psychological illnesses such as depression may prevent individuals from meeting this relational level of needs.

The highest two levels in the pyramid are self-actualization and self-transcendence. Self-actualization refers to realizing one's full potential—to do all that one can do. This can look very different for each individual depending on his or her personal goals. For example, one person may experience this need as being the perfect parent, while another may feel that it is artistic expression that fulfills their goals. Finally, self-transcendence is the need to align oneself with some higher goal outside of oneself, such as service to others or devoting time to mindful, spiritual practices.

# Societal Goals

Of course, as individuals we are heavily influenced by the conditions of the society in which we live, and as active citizens and community participants, we feel an obligation to contribute to the larger goals of society as best we can, and raise our children to do the same.

Additionally, as the world is becoming increasingly interconnected, our social goals must expand to broader levels of awareness, complexity, and scale, as we now need to consider how we affect others both face-to-face and virtually. Just as Socrates viewed "society as the soul writ large,"[19] at the scale of global humanity, our wider societal goals can be seen as parallel to the general progression of personal goals outlined in Maslow's Pyramid of Needs.

At the lower levels, it is important that the human species and the other species we depend on for our existence, all thrive. We must have the security to know that our food supply will not run out, our social systems will not collapse, and so on. At the higher levels, we strive to fulfill our collective potential – developing socially and technologically, overcoming prejudices, gathering the best possible scientific information and acting on it, and so on.

One may argue that at the highest level, the need is to achieve a species-wide feeling of relatedness and cohesion, with every individual and every group contributing their part, with the resulting chorus much greater and more harmonious than the sum of its individual voices.

In contrast, societal goals are often traditionally discussed in economic terms, related to growth and prosperity, as measured by the gross domestic product (GDP). In theory, this measure should reflect other kinds of progress as well, showing how well people are able to contribute to their societies, and how countries

---

[19] Plato, *Plato in Twelve Volumes*, Vols. 5 and 6, trans. by Paul Shorey (Cambridge, MA: Harvard University Press, 1969).

are becoming more successful. Yet this economic measure clearly has its limitations (such as not directly including the health of citizens or the environment as significant factors) and we are beginning to shift to measures of broader indicators such as well-being, as we realize we must not limit ourselves by what is easiest to measure, but instead focus on what matters for personal and societal fulfillment.

The OECD (Organization for Economic Co-operation and Development based in Paris) has created the Better Life Initiative,[20] an online tool in which people are invited to create their own index of well-being by prioritizing these 11 topics: community, education, environment, civic engagement, health, housing, income, jobs, life satisfaction, safety, work–life balance.

The UN has created the Sustainable Development Goals, which define the seventeen areas for growth by 2030, with measurable outcomes (more detail on their website).[21]

---

[20] Better Life Initiative, www.oecdbetterlifeindex.org

[21] United Nations, "Sustainable Development Goals," https://sustainabledevelopment.un.org/topics

Figure 2.2 Sustainable Development Goals
*Source:* @theglobalgoals (Instagram)

Another set of indicators, The Social Progress Index, measures countries' performance on three dimensions: basic human needs (nutrition and medical care, water and sanitation, shelter, and personal safety), foundations of wellbeing (access to basic knowledge, access to information and communication, health and wellness, and ecosystem sustainability), and opportunity (personal rights, personal freedom and choice, tolerance and inclusion, and access to advanced education).[22]

---

[22] Social Progress Index,
http://www.socialprogressimperative.org/data/spi/definitions

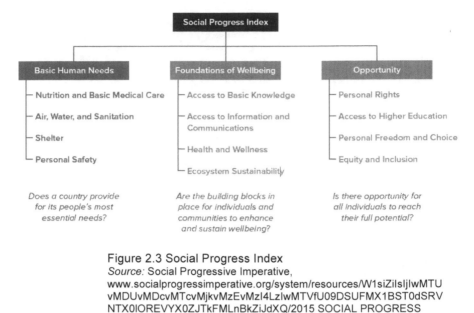

Figure 2.3 Social Progress Index
*Source:* Social Progressive Imperative,
www.socialprogressimperative.org/system/resources/W1siZiIsIjlwMTU
vMDUvMDcvMTcvMjkvMzEvMzI4LzIwMTVfU09DSUFMX1BST0dSRV
NTX0IOREVYX0ZJTkFMLnBkZiJdXQ/2015 SOCIAL PROGRESS
INDEX_FINAL.pdf

The Good Country Index measures how much each country contributes in seven areas[23] globally. Still others incorporate happiness as a distinct measure of societal success.[24] The question underlying all of these measures of the health and well-being of our societies is:

*How will we learn to strive for not only economic growth but also social progress and overall well-being?*

This is a question that all twenty-first century decision makers and students will need to learn how to answer in ever-more innovative and sophisticated ways.

So, are the goals of education situated at the individual or at the societal level? This is really a false dichotomy. Consider the dynamic of the race between technology and education described

---

[23] Science and technology, culture, international peace and security, world order, planet and climate, prosperity and equality, and health and well-being. www.goodcountry.org/overall

[24] For example, Bhutan's Gross National Happiness Index, www.gnhc.gov.bt/ and the Happy Planet Index: www.happyplanetindex.org

in the previous section. When education lags behind technology, individuals cannot meet workforce needs, and society and individuals suffer as a result, with income inequality, productivity losses, and increased social instability. The goals of the individual are closely tied to the goals of society and vice versa.

In the ideal case, all the individuals within each society (and the global society) have their physiological, safety, belonging, esteem, self-actualization, and self-transcendence needs met, and the society itself is thriving and meeting all of its needs, with each level enhancing the others. This ideal case is in fact the overarching purpose for education in society.

# Education Goals

How does formal education address the goals of individuals and society? There are four common educational services provided by formal K–12 education systems, all of which provide value and benefits to society's citizens.

### 1. Child Care
Rather than have each family apply their own resources alone to take care of their own children, education aggregates this task and provides important daily child care services for families.

### 2. Socialization
By engaging with others, students learn basic social skills through myriads of self-managed social interactions. These relationship experiences build the foundation for learning more complex socio-emotional skills and character qualities.

### 3. Accreditation and Evaluation
The seal of approval of the formal education system, which is intended to be a signal to others of one's successful completion of similar learning experiences, provides a degree of standardization

and quality control for identifying one's levels of core knowledge.

## 4. Education Goals, Standards, and Curricula

The common canonical set of knowledge, skills, and other competencies, and how they are intended to be learned, are all designed to provide students a foundational understanding of relevant subjects and essential skills, which in turn helps them succeed in the world and binds societies together with shared understandings and references, and a common educational foundation. This is necessary for both individual fulfillment, and a thriving society.

The last item—education goals, standards, and curricula—is the focus of our work and this book. In order for education to be effective in meeting the needs and goals of individuals and society, the core canonical set of education principles and practices must be aligned with the personal development of individuals, the challenges of society, and the shifting needs of local and global workforces.

For individuals, it must nurture their development across Maslow's Pyramid, providing places of safety, social connections, and protected experimentation, allowing all individuals to find their passions and larger roles in society and the world.

For society, students must be prepared for the demands of the world by learning useful and relevant knowledge, skills, character qualities, and meta-learning strategies. In the twenty-first century, these societal needs are shifting rapidly. For example, instead of having three television channels everyone can be sure almost everyone else has watched, we now have a sea of constantly expanding online content, spreading through social media. And yet, students around the world, having never met, find themselves sharing a common language of memes, ideas and references. It is the job of standards and curricula to instill the competencies necessary for people to choose content that has depth, and to approach it intelligently. We must realign education goals, standards, and curricula to reflect our changing knowledge and the dynamic transformations happening in our world.

Often, however, the need for accreditation and standardized testing can be in tension with shifting education goals, standards, and curricula. Accreditation often plays a large part in the creation of our sense of value of different fields, subjects, degrees, and the quality of institutional offerings. Instead of having to individually consider every aspect of every educational institution, parents and students rely on the quality control of accreditation systems to do this work for them. Brand names have become simple indicators of quality (especially at the higher education level), and serve as quick proxies for all the information parents and students really need to absorb to make good educational decisions.

This can have two significant consequences. Accreditation standards and the standardized testing of them, by necessity, create a focus on external goals of performance and a sorting mechanism of students, which can run counter to the goal of personal mastery of learning. If students are being externally judged on their performance, and the outcomes affect their future opportunities, standardized testing and accreditation can reinforce extrinsic motivations, often undercutting intrinsic motivations for learning.

Additionally, accreditation factors can emphasize the marketplace function of educational institutions, with colleges and universities working toward the explicit goal of attracting candidates who will pay tuition (either directly or through student loans), and may contribute generous donations later in their careers. This economic focus of education, with students as customers and educational institutions as businesses, superimposed onto the social purposes of education systems, shifts the dynamics further away from personal mastery of learning competencies toward extrinsic goals (more on this in Chapter Six, "The Meta-Learning Dimension") and competition between students and among educational institutions.

# Education Evolving?

Despite the world transforming at unprecedented rates, education has been slow to change. The following is a graphic representation of the evolution of the main subjects taught in schools from ancient times to the present.

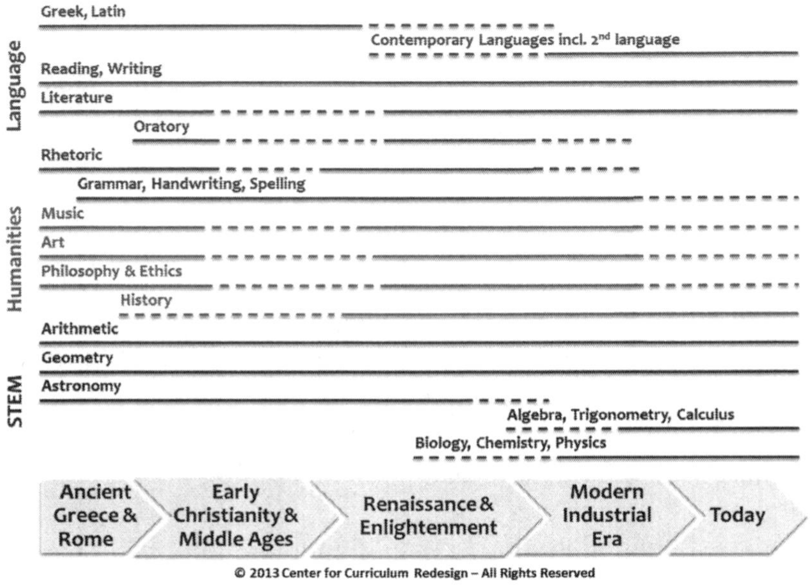

Figure 2.4 School Subjects Over Time
*Source:* CCR

Overall, while new subjects such as higher level mathematics and sciences have been added, and certain subjects such as rhetoric have been discarded, the core set of knowledge disciplines we have been passing on and teaching students has remained remarkably consistent.

One of the main obstacles in changing the goals, standards, and curricula of education is historical inertia. Even as we re-awaken to the importance of a variety of competencies beyond basic knowledge and skills, it is difficult to effectively insert new subjects and skills into an already established and content-crowded system. Ambitious innovation becomes nearly impossible under such constraints. In most cases, new goals and content additions are tacked on to an already overburdened curriculum, and with the pressure of preparing for standardized tests, relatively few educators are able to consistently provide the time needed to effectively integrate new learning goals into the curriculum.

So what are the mechanisms of this inertia?

At the policy level, most countries must work with an inherent level of instability, with elections and changes of leadership occurring every few years. The frequent changes of personnel (at both the staff level and the ministerial level), and the political pressures to balance the competing interests of voters, parents, unions, businesses, and so on, often preclude the continuity necessary to reflect on large-scale trends, plan for long-term goals, take calculated risks, or embrace change and innovation.

At the level of human expertise and authority, decisions are often reserved for subject-matter experts. These experts' opinions are partial and biased in certain predictable ways. First, experts feel responsible for upholding earlier standards, as they have sometimes been part of creating them and promoting their benefits. Being loyal to their field of study, they also find it difficult to discard parts of the whole cloth of their field's knowledge, even after those parts have become outdated or less useful. And their field looms more important in their eyes than any other.

Second, it is also very difficult for experts to add new disciplines to traditional fields of knowledge. For example, algorithmics and game theory are topics that are relevant for current advancements in a variety of fields that use mathematics, but tradition-oriented mathematics experts do not include them in their efforts to reform mathematics curriculum. Additionally, expert academics often operate in relative isolation from the demands of the real world, sometimes unaware of the ways their discipline is currently being applied in professional settings outside academia.

Finally, these subject-matter experts place a large emphasis on the ways others in their field around the world are accomplishing similar curriculum reviews. In trying to adjust to emulate the others, they are subject to groupthink, and together they are rarely able to be highly innovative.

Successful implementation of the CCR education goals will hinge on two critical factors that address these challenges. At the policy level, we will need to strive toward a stable consensus among political factions, and a clearly articulated vision of the kind of education students now need. At the level of disciplinary experts, there needs to be continuous involvement of real-world users of the disciplines, in addition to reform-minded academics.

We will need to leverage best practices from education systems around the world (and from industry where applicable). We will need to carefully re-examine the relevance of what we teach, curate the traditional disciplines, add relevant modern disciplines, and place emphasis on more holistic learning—not just knowledge but also skills, character, and meta-learning. Finally, we will need the courage to innovate, letting go of the comfort of an existing system and working under conditions of uncertainty toward a better one.

# Key Qualities of a Twenty-First Century Curriculum

> If we teach today's students as we taught yesterday's, we rob them of tomorrow.
> —John Dewey

## Adaptability

In the natural world, organisms that are a good fit for the new environment survive, and those that are unfit die off. This is the central tenet of natural selection.

Less often discussed, however, is how species are able to survive across changes in environment, by evolving the capability to be adaptable. The Great Tit (*Parus major*), a small bird that lives a very short lifespan, is an example of a species that has a high chance of long-term survival, even with drastic changes in their environment. They are behaviorally versatile, laying their eggs at the optimal moment based on the conditions around them, and as a species they evolve rapidly, keeping pace with environmental changes on a collective level.[25]

We humans have not only survived, but also flourished to the point of reaching a number of limits of our global resources, due to our incredible adaptability. We developed tools, refined them, learned to control our food by planting and replanting the seeds of the most useful plants, and then spread these innovations around the world. We've learned to mass produce products, set up systems of organized work and self-governance and are weaving a global web of information and communications. Our technological breakthroughs have allowed us to settle all over the world, and overcome genetic differences that were historically fatal for our ancestors. We were able to do all this because our brains have evolved to be very large and are constantly being reshaped by the environment around us. While other animals are born with many abilities, such as walking, humans are helpless for a relatively long portion of development. This helps to ensure that each human being will become optimally tuned to fit its environment and culture, as their brains adapt to whatever their surroundings happens to demand. Versatility is the key to survival in a changing world; it is true for the species, and it is thus true for curriculum— the shared base of understanding and competency of our species.

If a curriculum is not adaptive, it becomes rigid. There is no such thing as a perfect curriculum that does not need updating, because the world continues to change and the goals of an optimal curriculum changes with it. Depending on the subject, the change can happen at different rates. For example, relevant programming languages change every two years, but ancient philosophy remains much more constant. This does not mean that the curriculum should fall victim to fads, but rather that there should be built-in

[25] Oscar Vedder, Sandra Bouwhuis, and Ben C. Sheldon, "Quantitative Assessment of the Importance of Phenotypic Plasticity in Adaptation to Climate Change in Wild Bird Populations," *PLoS Biology* 11, no. 7 (2013), doi: 10.1371/journal.pbio.1001605

mechanisms for keeping the curriculum up to date with modern findings and new breakthroughs.

Another aspect of the adaptability of curriculum is its potential to take place outside of the classroom and virtually, on computer screens, from anywhere in the world. For some important learning goals, the classroom is not the optimal learning environment, and there are now many opportunities for deep and rich learning beyond the classroom walls. These informal opportunities include a wide variety of after-school programs (such as clubs, scouting, etc.), museums, virtual field trips, online learning programs, digital micro-certifications and learning badges, internships, apprenticeships, community service learning, and much more.

A truly adaptable, twenty-first century curriculum is never finished or complete for two reasons. First, humanity's knowledge base continues to grow and change, and curriculum must constantly change in order to stay current. This book itself is an adaptable, living document, subject to revision and change as we learn more about what the world is becoming, what it needs, and the best ways to achieve our individual and collective goals through education.

Second, it is important to reserve adaptable portions that can be tailored to each individual student's needs, their interests, and personal growth goals. Personal control of one's learning has been shown to be crucial to students' motivation and positive learning outcomes as well as for developing one's executive functions,[26] and is itself an important lifelong learning strategy. An effective curriculum provides learners with a solid introduction to different bodies of knowledge, highlighting key concepts, processes, methods, and tools. It also highlights the relevant practical, cognitive, and emotional aspects of those engaged in developing that knowledge and applying it in the world, so students are equipped to choose which fields to study and continue to refine their own career choices throughout their lives.

---

[26] J. E. Barker et al., "Less-Structured Time In Children's Daily Lives Predicts Self-Directed Executive Functioning," *Frontiers in Psychology* 5 (2014).

In this way, learning continues throughout a person's life, with less and less material being prescribed top-down, and more and more of it chosen and managed by the learner. The graph below illustrates this desired dynamic for control of instructional time over a lifespan.[27] By following this dynamic from the moment students enter school, the curriculum provides learning scaffolds early on, removes them when they are no longer needed, and enables students to continue their learning, driven by their own interests, well after formal schooling ends.

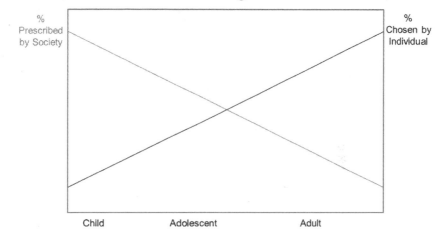

Figure 2.5 Developmental Shifting of Control of Instructional Time
*Source:* CCR

# Balance

When trying to make sense of the complex set of our education needs, the immense variety of perspectives on the conditions of education today, and the plethora of theories and practices related to learning, it is not uncommon to fall victim to a mindset of false choices, such as: "Which is better?"—teaching knowledge, or teaching skills? Should education focus on the humanities, or on science, technology, engineering, and

---

[27] Student-driven activities such as play are not included, but are very important.

mathematics (STEM)? Should schools develop character qualities or help students pass important high-stakes tests?

In this book we take a firm stance against these false dichotomies. We believe that in order for a twenty-first century curriculum to be truly holistic, it must incorporate and balance the various goals of education. The following are just a few examples.

### 1. Modern Knowledge and Traditional Subjects

Modern subjects such as robotics, entrepreneurship, coding, and media communications need to be introduced, and yet traditional subjects such as reading, mathematics and language are still foundational. We must carefully comb through the existing curricula to remove obsolete units and sections in order to make room for the relevant modern topics and themes, but this does not mean a wholesale abandonment of existing curricula. It does however imply a deep redesign of them.

### 2. Depth and Breadth

Although there is a limited amount of school time, we believe that it is crucial that the curriculum both encourages depth (expertise in specific knowledge domains) and breadth (overview and high level understanding of the knowledge landscape of various subject areas). Students should be encouraged to make connections across topics as they dive deeply into a selection of them.

### 3. Science, Technology, Engineering, and Math (STEM) and Humanities

Although there is a lot of demand for STEM-related jobs, versatility is always a good hedge against future uncertainty. Well-designed humanities and arts programs, implemented successfully, can teach many of the skills required for success in a wide variety of careers (critical thinking, creativity, etc.).

Arts education has been linked to higher creative thinking, improved perceptions of the self as a learner, more positive school climates, and much more.[28] To quote Steve Jobs, "Technology alone is not enough... it's technology married with liberal arts, married with humanities, that yield the results that make our hearts sing."

## 4. The Mind and The Body

As the ancient saying goes, *"mens sana in corpore sano"* (a healthy mind in a healthy body). Including opportunities to develop nutritional health, exercise, good sleeping habits, relaxation and mindfulness training, sports and athletics, etc., have all shown positive benefits for learning, motivation and self-development. Because our minds are intricately connected to our bodies, it is important to recognize the feedback loop that exists, and not neglect either aspect.

## 5. Knowledge, Skills, Character, and Meta-Learning

Traditionally, the main focus of an educational curriculum has been on learning content knowledge. But a growing body of research from a wide range of fields has pointed to the need for students to balance content knowledge and understanding with skills that apply that knowledge to the real world; character qualities that build motivation, resilience, and social/emotional intelligence; and meta-learning

---

[28] J. Burton, R. Horowitz, and H. Abeles, "Learning In and Through the Arts: Curriculum Implications," in *Champions of Change: The Impact of the Arts on Learning*, The Arts Education Partnership, 1999, 35–46, http://files.eric.ed.gov/fulltext/ED435581.pdf

strategies that help students become reflective, self-directed, and expert learners.

## 6. Outcome and Process

Too often, the performance aspect of education causes emphasis to be placed on the outcome of educational experiences, rather than the processes that led to them. For students, being rewarded only for the outcome can undermine intrinsic motivation (or a growth/mastery/learning mindset), especially because the process is often difficult and not smooth. The reaction to this trend, then, is to focus entirely on process, placing no emphasis on outcome (often accomplished by eliminating grades or expectations entirely). This can lead to students failing to meet expectations of broader society (like college admissions) and being unprepared to build on what they have learned. It is important that both outcome and process are highlighted as important parts of the learning process, and that both are rewarded.

## 7. Personal and Societal Goals and Needs

It is tempting to pose the question: Should I do what is best for me, or what is best for my community/society? However, as discussed above, it is not necessary to choose one or the other. Individuals' goals and societies' goals can often work in concert in such a way that each enhances the other. Ideally, people find or create a job that makes use of their talents, that aligns with their passions, and that helps to improve the world.

## 8. Global and Local Perspectives

Although our framework focuses on a global perspective for a unifying framework, it leaves room, intentionally, for each local community to determine for themselves what is important to include from their local perspectives. We want everyone to benefit from the insights of common goals, without letting these common goals interfere with local values and understandings in a disruptive way. Ideally these work together to create an outcome that is better than one informed just by global (top–down) or just local (bottom-up) ideas. The framework can be a guiding document to help empower individuals and countries at the local and global levels.

## 9. Deeply Internalized and Flexible

In order for this framework to be effective, it must be deeply internalized and used to redesign current standards. However, this cannot lead to a rigid, unchanging new normal. Part of what must be internalized is the understanding that we must constantly change to adapt to changes in the world and our understanding.

## 10. Social Progress Ideals and Respect of Local Norms

We describe social progress as broadly applicable all around the world. At the large scale that deals with everyone having enough food and water, encouraging peace in our communities, and living sustainably, these are undeniably universally applicable. However, we must be careful to not be overly prescriptive at finer grained levels of detail. It is not true, for example, that personal assertiveness or achievement is always a positive quality to strive for—context and culture are important factors when considering social ideals. While we believe that there are globally relevant social progress ideals, we also believe it is

important to be respectful of local norms, and that
these two goals are not at odds.

How can education achieve all these goals, strike all these
balances, and support an integrated, whole-person approach to
learning that prepares every student for the demands of the twenty-
first century? To start with, a more integrated and unified
framework of learning goals and competencies is needed.

# A Unifying Framework of Educational Goals

If you have no idea where you want to go, it
makes little difference how fast you travel.
—Italian Proverb

## Why a New Education Framework?

In the world of education systems and reform, there is great
confusion as to which wording and what constructs should be used
as a common language. In Canada/Québec, for instance,
competencies are categorized as key/cross-curricular
competencies; subject-bound competencies, and lifelong-learning
competencies. In Guatemala they are divided into framework
competencies, area competencies, subject/strand competency, and
grade competencies. In Indonesia competency standards are being
developed in two categories—cross-cutting competencies and
subject-bound competencies, that in turn, are divided into standard
competencies (of a more general nature) and basic competencies
(as illustrations or specifications of the subject-bound standard
competencies).

According to UNESCO:[29] "Quality education systems have to enable learners to continuously adapt their competencies while continuously acquiring and even developing new ones. These competencies are diverse in scope ranging from core skills, content knowledge, cognitive skills, soft skills, to occupational skills and enable us to meet a complex demand or carry out a complex activity or task successfully or effectively in a certain context. Their typologies and approaches are as diverse as the entities—countries, organizations and individuals—that define them."

There is a growing consensus on the types of competencies needed, but a wide variety of formulations and organizational schemes for these core competencies are shown in Table 2.1.

| UK/Ireland | Norway | Scotland | Australia | New Zealand |
|---|---|---|---|---|
| Skills:<br><br>Communication.<br><br>Personal and interpersonal skills.<br><br>Manage information. | Pursuit of five basic skills:<br><br>Being able to express oneself.<br><br>Being able to express oneself in writing.<br><br>Being able to use digital tools.<br><br>Being able to read.<br><br>Being able to develop numeracy.<br><br>Being able to use digital tools. | Pursuit of four main capacities:<br><br>Successful learners.<br><br>Confident individuals.<br><br>Responsible citizens.<br><br>Effective contributors.<br><br>Literacy.<br><br>Health and wellbeing.<br><br>Skills of learning, life, and work.<br><br>Literacy.<br><br>Numeracy. | Ten capabilities:<br><br>Literacy.<br><br>Thinking skills.<br><br>Creativity.<br><br>Self-Management.<br><br>Teamwork.<br><br>Intercultural Understanding.<br><br>Ethical behavior and social competence.<br><br>Literacy.<br><br>Numeracy.<br><br>ICT.<br><br>Thinking skills.<br><br>Creativity. | Five key competencies:<br><br>Use language, symbols, and text.<br><br>Manage self.<br><br>Relate to others.<br><br>Participate and contribute.<br><br>Thinking. |

---

[29] UNESCO, www.unesco.org/new/en/education/themes/strengthening-education-systems/quality-framework/desired-outcomes/competencies

Note: Table 2.1 continued from previous page.

| Indonesia | Singapore | Namibia | South Africa |
|---|---|---|---|
| National examinations will target:<br><br>Intelligence.<br><br>Knowledge.<br><br>Personality.<br><br>Noble character.<br><br>Skills to live by independently.<br><br>Skills to continue studies. | Core skills and values:<br><br>Communication skills.<br><br>Character development.<br><br>Self-management skills.<br><br>Social and cooperative skills.<br><br>Thinking skills and creativity.<br><br>Literacy and numeracy.<br><br>Information skills.<br><br>Knowledge application skills. | Learning to learn.<br><br>Personal skills.<br><br>Social skills.<br><br>Cognitive skills.<br><br>Communication skills.<br><br>Numeracy skills.<br><br>Information and communication technology skills. | Identify and solve problems<br><br>Work effectively with others<br><br>Collect, analyze, organize, and critically evaluate information.<br><br>Communicate effectively.<br><br>Use science and technology effectively.<br><br>Demonstrate understanding of the world as a set of related systems.<br><br>Full personal development (reflecting on and exploring strategies to learn more effectively, responsible citizens, cultural and aesthetical sensitiveness, education for career and entrepreneurial opportunities). |

Table 2.1 Core Competencies
*Source:* UNESCO, www.unesco.org/new/en/education/themes/strengthening-education-systems/quality-framework/technical-notes/examples-of-countries-definitions-of-competencies/

Research in cognitive science and education is similarly broad, with different schools of thought using different terms. In trying to apply research to education, there is a tension between precision and clarity. When experts write about their findings, their goal is to be as precise as possible. The assumptions of each concept are tested and refined, and more detailed models are built to more deeply understand educational competencies, such as critical thinking, creativity, mindfulness, and so on. While extremely detailed models are important for nuanced research questions, they are often difficult to use as insights for actionable, everyday decisions in teaching and learning.

The purpose of the framework of educational goals presented here is to synthesize existing research and best practices while maximizing accuracy, clarity, and usefulness, leveraging all the most important findings without getting bogged down in the fine-grain distinctions.[30] The goal is to learn from all of our experience and to help make the design goals of a twenty-first century education easier to understand and implement. From there, educators will be better equipped to engage in the essential, long-term work of redesigning and transforming education systems, and researchers will be better equipped to ask more relevant, accurate questions, so we may all make our educational decisions as up-to-date and informed as possible.

It may be helpful to think of this framework as similar to the evolution of the Food Pyramid in two ways.

---

[30] For a discussion of CCR's logic behind the chosen terminology, see Appendix.

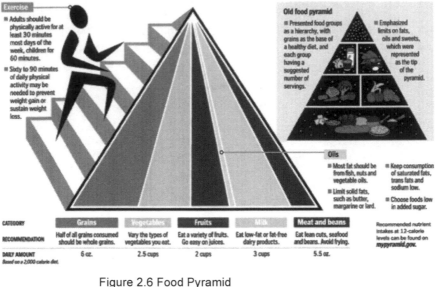

Figure 2.6 Food Pyramid
*Source:* The Washington Post Company

The first is that we are laying out the broad strokes of a healthy learning diet for all students. Of course the daily learning nutrition for each student must be tailored to the student's age, interests, culture, values, and so on. We are not prescribing specific activities, just as the food pyramid does not prescribe specific meals or recipes; it simply recommends eating certain amounts in each food group, such as vegetables, grains, fruits. For education, this translates to certain proportions of learning in each of the categories of the framework. Second, like the food pyramid, this framework is meant to change over time based on new information about how we learn best and what kinds of learning are most needed.

# Our Theory of Change

There are many aspects of education systems that influence the quality of learning in a particular school or classroom: socio-economic status, school culture, professional development, teacher quality, pressure from standardized tests, and the list goes on. For every factor, there are many related reform efforts aimed at improving teaching and student outcomes, and these vary in approach and effectiveness. Here we ask a different question:

Knowing what we know about how children learn and what is necessary for individuals and societies to succeed and thrive, *what* should students be learning?

Many teachers are already teaching toward the goals we set forth here, and many are not. Our hope is to create a framework that can serve as the foundation for deep discussions about our educational design goals and how well we are achieving them. Assessment drives change in education, and we believe that it is crucial to be aligned and measuring the right things, so that educators can teach in an environment that supports and rewards deep learning across the framework of what needs to be learned (see "About CCR—CCR's Assessment Research Consortium" at the end of the book for more details).

Educators who have reviewed this framework sometimes ask, "Why aren't you including in your efforts a particular focus on students who are struggling in various ways—low socio-economic status, learning differences, and so on?"

We believe these are very important issues, and that there will be a wide variety of ways to adapt and modify learning practices for each learner no matter where they are on the spectra of individual learner needs. CCR is stimulating change at the systemic level, for *all* students, by working with influential stakeholders (such as the OECD) in creating a framework that is robust, comprehensive and adaptable for all.

By creating a framework of educational goals, we can influence the discussion about standards for education, and how standards will pave the way for crafting the deep re-design of assessments to make them more holistic and relevant. When assessments reflect updated views on what is important to learn, it will be necessary to redesign curriculum to align with the new assessment approaches, and concurrently, professional development to prepare educators to help students learn the updated curricula, as shown here:

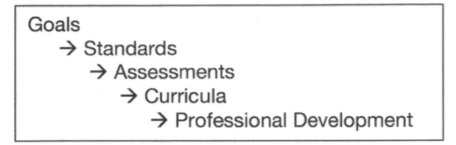

Figure 2.7 Professional Development
*Source:* CCR

Of course, there are feedback loops from each level to each of the other levels in this model. Education is a large and complicated system, which is why we need to take a step back, look at the big picture, and be intentional with how we approach this historic education challenge.

Progress will be staggered. When renovating a house, it is important to drastically change only one section at a time, while living in the other sections. In trying to change a large entity like the education system, we must understand that it will not happen all at once. Both the *what* (standards and assessment), and the *how* (curriculum and professional development) need to change over time.

The CCR is now focused on the first two rooms of renovation—standards and assessment. We are focusing on these levels in order to eventually effect change across all levels; as the saying goes, "what gets counted ends up counting." It will then be up to individual countries and jurisdictions as to how specific progress will be made on the curriculum and professional development, in ways that are aligned and harmonious with the updated education goals, standards, and assessments, and are best suited to the specific style, needs, and values of each education system.[31]

---

[31] The CCR does not recommend a single view, but does encourage thorough understanding of one's perspective and the larger whole that includes the perspectives of others.

In addition to the four areas of standards, assessments, curricula and professional development, there is often, in many jurisdictions, a silent influence that has gone mostly unchallenged: College entrance requirements. Such requirements, with their entrance tests, have been constructed to ascertain the student's ability to succeed in university courses, mostly from a traditional knowledge perspective. They very rarely, if ever, reflect skills, character, and the meta-learning abilities of the student, and are not a predictor for life success outside academia. They very often bias the requirements of school systems, in deciding for instance how much algebra should be required irrespective of how useful it may be, and not realizing that it is really a sorting mechanism based on a proxy to tenacity.[32] As this realization starts to sink in, jurisdictions such as British Columbia[33] are challenging their higher education environments to deeply rethink their entrance requirements. More research, analysis, concentration, and innovative problem-solving are needed to understand how to address the need of higher education to fairly sort applicants, yet assess the full individual, and most critically, not hold back progress in transforming education standards and assessment systems.

## The CCR Process

As an independent, non-partisan, international organization, the Center for Curriculum Redesign (CCR) uses an evidence- and research-based process for developing and refining its frameworks. This process draws from three distinct collaborative efforts: synthesis, analysis, and organization.

---

[32] D. Silver, M. Saunders, and E. Zarate, *What Factors Predict High School Graduation in the Los Angeles Unified School District* (Santa Barbara, CA: California Dropout Research Project, UCLA, 2008); also see C. Adelman, *The Toolbox Revisited: Paths to Degree Completion from High School Through College* (Washington, DC: U.S. Department of Education, 2006).
[33] Global Education Leader's Partnership, http://gelponline.org/gelp-community/jurisdictions/british-columbia

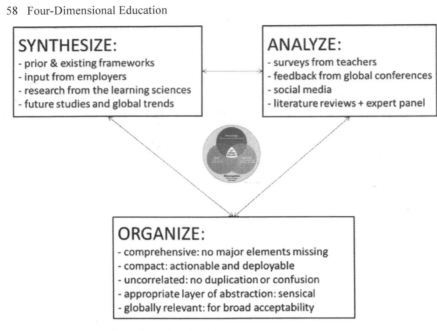

Figure 2.8 The CCR Process
*Source:* CCR

## Synthesize

The CCR recognizes that a lot of work has already been done already in identifying promising areas of education reform. In order to not reinvent the wheel, the CCR uses meta-syntheses on prior and existing frameworks developed by jurisdictions and national bodies (such as ministries of education), professional bodies (such as the National Council of Teachers of Mathematics) and organizations (such as P21.org). It also draws from analyses of employers' needs (such as an IBM study of 15,000 CEOs from 60 countries and 33 industries). The CCR also ensures that its concepts are current by constantly monitoring and synthesizing research from the learning sciences and by aligning itself with analyses of global trends and future studies.

## Analyze

The CCR believes in the importance of collaboration with relevant parties in the creation of a framework that will support them in their goals. To do so, we have gathered feedback from over 600 teachers from around the world, and held international conferences and colloquia on issues discussed in the framework (such as mathematics, character, metacognition, employability etc.). The CCR also will begin to gather information via social media regarding what students and parents want from their education. Finally, the CCR conducts specific literature reviews and draws from experts from a global network of thought leaders and partnering organizations (such as the OECD).

## Organize

As the CCR draws from so many sources, it is crucial that the final product be *accurate* and *actionable*. The CCR framework aims to accomplish this using the following five design goals:

### 1. Comprehensive

This attribute is the most self-explanatory. It is not enough to create a framework for a subset of the educational goals one hopes to achieve (for example, only skills). Education suffers from an overabundance of programs attempting to fix a single aspect of education. No one approach is a silver bullet, and one needs to think carefully and holistically about education as a system. Furthermore, by focusing on just one aspect at a time, discussions become polarized and force a choice between aspects of the current education system. It is crucial to not leave out any important ideas, so that others who have been thinking of similar concepts in different formulations are able to see the ways in which their thinking can be mapped onto our framework. For example, resilience (a character quality), includes the concepts of grit, perseverance, and so on. By creating a framework that is comprehensive, the CCR is hoping to organize all of the high-level thinking about education design, so everyone can consider how the different elements interact and fit together.

## 2. **Compact**

As described above, it is a difficult task to synthesize research in a way that makes the conclusions actionable, yet keeps them accurate. Frameworks that attempt to include all of the nuances of the research literature end up being too difficult to deploy, realistically. Miller's law from psychology states that people can remember only seven (plus or minus two) items in their working memories, but they can chunk items into groups, thus remembering more items using a hierarchical structure, with the maximum remaining seven plus or minus two. Our framework therefore has *four* categories, each containing fewer than seven components. This ensures that the framework is concise enough to be memorable and thus actionable.

## 3. **Uncorrelated**

In reality, many of the goals of education (creativity, optimism, courage, etc.) are correlated to various degrees. That is, someone who is optimistic may also be more likely to have zest, compared to someone who is not optimistic. Research into these concepts often tries to isolate the effects of each factor to understand its importance. To synthesize these different constructs, most correlated items are grouped together, and least correlated items (or uncorrelated, or anti-correlated) are kept separate. Questions guiding this process include: Is it possible to have one without the other? How often does that happen? Has research shown a relationship? That way, each concept is important on its own, and its importance is not mostly captured in another concept, making it more confusing to think of each one independently.

This clears up confusion that results from different constructs having different origins and overlapping definitions. For example, by separating meta-learning into its own dimension, decision-making is removed from the realm of critical thinking. Now it suggests that one uses all of her knowledge, skills (including critical thinking), and character qualities when making decisions. Linguistic and ontological perfection is illusory, because the concepts all interact to various degrees. The ultimate goal, however, is for the concepts to be a useful grouping that reflects how these ideas are used in everyday learning and for educators to keep them as helpful checklists in their educational practices.

### 4. **Appropriate**

People naturally think of the world in a variety of ways and at a variety of levels. Tying one's shoelaces and learning how to learn are both referred to as skills, but at very different layers of abstraction. Clearly, it's important for our students to be good people, and it's also important that they know how to add. In this framework, goals and concepts are placed in a sensible way according to their level of abstraction, and their origin. So, addition and ethics belong in different dimensions and in different levels of the framework. Low-level mechanical skills (e.g., multiplication) are in subcategories according to their relevant academic knowledge concepts, while ethics is in a category at a higher level, under character qualities. In this way, the framework becomes a foundation for clear discussions that respect the complexity of the many related variables relevant to each educational component.

### 5. **Globally Relevant**

As the world is increasing in connectivity, it becomes more important to be mindful of cultural differences and the spectrum of deeper human goals and connections. The CCR framework is meant to be broad and deep enough to not be culture-dependent, but rather to provide a common understanding for effective cross-cultural communication. The ideas discussed here are relevant to everyone in the world who will be participating in constructing the future together. All countries, then, can use this framework and customize it according to their own values and needs.

The CCR framework synthesizes existing research with the overarching complementary goals of maximizing both accuracy and clarity. This leverages all the findings from scholarly research and exemplary practice without getting bogged down in hair-splitting, endless academic debates. By establishing a framework that incorporates the foundational work that has been done on these topics, and formulating it in a clear way, the design goals of education become crisper and provide a common ground for engaging in meaningful work toward redesigning education. On the cognitive science side, the questions that need more empirical research become clearer, so that educators may make their educational decisions as informed as possible.

Is CCR's framework radical or incremental? We prefer to call it "incrementally ambitious": if it were too radical, it would stand no chance of being adopted, given how complicated it is to modify the course of the formal education system. But if it is too incremental, it will continue missing the mark on what is relevant and needed for this century. The analogy is that of a butterfly compared to its caterpillar: they both share the same DNA, but clearly the butterfly has befitted from a substantial transformation—it has become unrecognizable as a caterpillar yet reflects the foundational tenets.

Figure 2.9 Caterpillar to Butterfly
*Source:* Unknown. Retrieved from Google Images.

# Beyond Knowledge—A Twenty-First Century Competencies Framework

Curriculum, as it is traditionally conceived, consists mostly of content knowledge that students must learn. In the modern world, progress in scientific understanding and technological breakthroughs is adding more and more pieces of knowledge at faster and faster rates, piling onto students' already overburdened learning plates. According to E.O. Wilson, "We are drowning in information, while starving for wisdom. The world henceforth will be run by synthesizers, people able to put together the right information at the right time, think critically about it, and make important choices wisely."[34]

Knowledge is absolutely essential, but we must rethink what is relevant in each subject area and adapt the curriculum to reflect priorities of learning in both traditional and modern disciplines. There is also a growing consensus among employers who hire recent graduates, and from leaders in countries around the world, that our current, knowledge-focused curriculum does not

---

[34] Edward O. Wilson, *Consilience: The Unity of Knowledge* (New York: Vintage, 1999), 294.

adequately prepare students for today's workforce and world, much less tomorrow's, and that students should practice applying their knowledge using skills.

As for character qualities, it is clear that policymakers are beginning to see their importance as part of a formal education, although educators and employers have known this for a long time. Despite what is traditionally conceived of as progress (economic growth, material productivity, etc.), countries are now tracking other indicators of social progress and the level of their responses to local and global challenges (e.g., poverty, violence, corruption, sustainability). This highlights the need for students to develop and build positive character qualities in addition to the knowledge and skills most needed for success.

In order to deepen and enhance the learning in these three dimensions—knowledge, skills, and character qualities—there is an important additional fourth dimension needed for a fully comprehensive twenty-first century education: meta-learning (often called learning to learn—the internal processes by which we reflect on and adapt our learning). It is not enough to implicitly include this fourth dimension in all the other dimensions—its significance must be highlighted explicitly, so that we are constantly reminded to incorporate meta-learning strategies into the knowledge, skills, and character portions of our learning experiences, learning how to strive to improve no matter what goals we set for ourselves.

In collaboration with the OECD's Education 2030 project,[35] we tabulated, analyzed, and synthesized thirty-two frameworks[36] from around the world, and found that there is

---

[35] The OECD has launched a new initiative, "Education 2030: the OECD Key Competencies Framework". The OECD intends to further develop the competencies framework by conducting an in-depth international comparative curriculum analysis. This global framework project aims to support countries in re-thinking curriculum reform, to prioritize which competencies will be critical and relevant for students to develop for future.

[36] OECD Skills for Innovation, OECD DeSeCo, OECD Social & Emotional Skills, OECD PISA, OECD PIAAC, EU Reference Framework Key Competencies, UNESCO Global Citizenship Education, P21, ATC21S, Asia

general agreement on these four dimensions of goals for a 21$^{st}$ century education. Table 2.2 highlights the commonalities among some of the most significant frameworks, and shows CCR's framework in relation to those for comparison.

---

Society/CCSSO, Hewlett Foundation Deeper Learning Competencies, ACT WorkKeys (WK)–NCRC Plus–CWRC Skills Assessments, CPS Employability Assessment (EA), AAC&U Essential Learning Outcomes (LEAP), CCSSO— Innovation Lab Network (ILN) State Framework, National Work Readiness Credential, CAE College & Work Ready (CWRA) & Collegiate Learning Assessment (CLA), EnGauge, Character Counts! Coalition, CharacterEd.Net, Character Education Partnership, Facing History and Ourselves, KIPP Schools, Center for the Advancement of Ethics and Character, Collaborative for Academic, Social, and Emotional Learning, The Jubilee Center for Character and Virtues, Young Foundation, China Ministry of Education, Singapore Character and Moral Education (CME), South Korea Moral Education, Swedish National Agency for Education, Thailand Philosophy of Sufficiency Economy.

| CCR | OECD Skills for Innovation | OECD DeSeCo | EU Reference Framework Key Competencies | Hewlett Foundation Deeper Learning Competencies | P21.org | ATC21S |
|---|---|---|---|---|---|---|
| Knowledge. | Subject-based skills. | Using tools interactively. | Communication in foreign languages. Mathematics, science and technology. Digital competence. Entrepreneurship. | Academic content. | Mathematics. Science. Language—English. Languages—World. Economics, Geography, History, Government & Civics. Arts. Information Literacy. Media Literacy. ICT Literacy. | Information literacy. ICT literacy. |
| Skills. | Skills in thinking and creativity. | Interacting in heterogeneous groups. | Communication in the mother tongue. | Think critically and solve complex problems. Work collaboratively Communicate effectively. | Creativity. Critical Thinking. Communication. Collaboration. | Creativity and innovation. Critical thinking, problem solving, decision making. Communication. Collaboration (teamwork). |
| Character. | Behavioral and social skills; also social and emotional skills. | Acting autonomously. | Social and civic competences Sense of initiative Cultural awareness and expression. | Academic mindsets. | Flexibility & Adaptability Initiative & Self-direction. Social & Cross-cultural Skills. Productivity & Accountability. Leadership & Responsibility. | Life and career. Citizenship – local and global. Cultural awareness and competence. Personal & social responsibility. |
| Meta-Learning. | | Reflectiveness. | Learning to learn. | Learning to learn. | Reflect critically. | Learning how to learn, Metacognition. |

Table 2.2 Commonalities between Global Frameworks
*Source:* CCR

Figure 2.10 is a visual representation of the complete CCR framework that shows how the four dimensions interact with each other. The details and justification of the framework will be given in subsequent chapters.

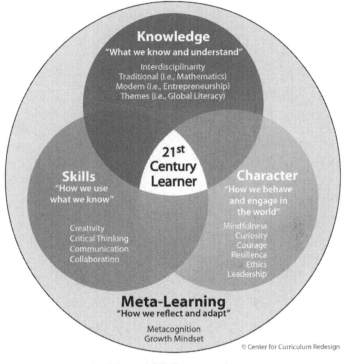

Figure 2.10 The CCR Framework
*Source:* CCR

In a classroom, these four dimensions are all intertwined, and effective learning is a rich blend of elements from all of them. For example, students might be asked to practice leadership and collaboration skills as they work in teams to develop robots (applying a wide variety of knowledge in science, technology, engineering, computer programming, and much more) that can solve a particular real-world problem, such as remotely sensing and extinguishing a small fire, and to be reflective of their learning progress throughout their project. In fact, the best learning experiences in schools around the world already integrate these different learning aspects, without necessarily referring to them explicitly.

We can design a matrix that shows the intersections of various knowledge areas (both traditional and modern), with the skills, character qualities, and meta-learning strategies that can be taught through them, as shown in Figure 2.11. Some areas of the matrix will be dense while others will be sparsely populated.

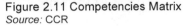

| © 2014 Center for Curriculum Redesign - All Rights Reserved | | | Skills | | | | | | Character | | | | | | Meta-Learning | |
| --- | --- | --- | --- | --- | --- | --- | --- | --- | --- | --- | --- | --- | --- | --- | --- | --- |
| | | Creativity | Critical thinking | Communication | Collaboration | Mindfulness | Curiosity | Courage | Resilience | Ethics | Leadership | Growth | Metacognition |
| Traditional Knowledge (Interdisciplinary) | | | | | | | | | | | | | |
| Mathematics | | | | | | | | | | | | | |
| Science | | | | | | | | | | | | | |
| Language | | | | | | | | | | | | | |
| Etc. | | | | | | | | | | | | | |
| Modern Knowledge (Interdisciplinary) | | | | | | | | | | | | | |
| Robotics | | | | | | | | | | | | | |
| Entrepreneurship | | | | | | | | | | | | | |
| Wellness | | | | | | | | | | | | | |
| Etc. | | | | | | | | | | | | | |
| Global literacy | | | | | | | | | | | | | |
| Environmental Literacy | | | | | | | | | | | | | |
| Etc. | | | | | | | | | | | | | |
| Themes - embedded throughout | | | | | | | | | | | | | |

Figure 2.11 Competencies Matrix
*Source:* CCR

The purpose here is to organize the existing, overwhelmingly large landscape of educational goals, and create a clear and useful way of thinking about curriculum. By identifying the dimensions, we have set up a clear structure for further conversation. Using this as a guiding framework, and mapping on the ways others have thought about education in the past, we can begin to deeply re-examine curricula.

Each knowledge discipline has a responsibility to include the learning of the skills, character qualities, and meta-learning strategies that are most aligned with it. For example, mathematics may be well suited to teaching critical thinking, resilience, and metacognition. Many of these competencies will not be offered as independent courses or modules in a school's curricular offerings, and must be intentionally interwoven into the relevant parts of existing learning activities. In fact, it is likely that they are generally best learned when grounded in the context of concrete knowledge domains.

Of course, all students' learning experiences will contribute to their development across these dimensions, and some of these learning goals (such as courage) may be more effectively addressed in out-of-school programs and experiences. Additionally, this matrix will look very different for children at different stages of their learning, although the core dimensions and their elements would remain the same.

We are not claiming to introduce entirely new ideas, as many of these learning goals go back to Socrates and Confucius. Rather, as discussed earlier, it is to organize and synthesize the overwhelmingly large landscape of educational goals, and create a more concise, clear, useful, relevant, and prioritized way of organizing what is now important to learn. By identifying the four dimensions and their elements, we are building a shared language for deeper conversations on how education should be transformed for our times.

Using this framework as a modern guide to what students now need to learn, and mapping the ways others have thought about education in the past to this framework, we can begin to deeply re-examine the dimensions of what is worth learning in the twenty-first century.

# Chapter 3

# The Knowledge Dimension

## Knowledge—Traditional and Modern

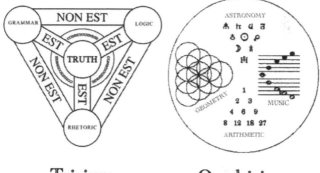

Trivium                    Quadrivium

## Evolving Maps of Traditional Knowledge Disciplines

Attempts to synthesize all of the disciplines of knowledge that were important for an educated person to learn date back to the sixth century. The most influential of early Western[37] formulations were the Trivium and Quadrivium—a medieval revival of classical

---

[37] During 2016, CCR will also synthesize Eastern traditions for curriculum.

Greek education theories that defined the seven liberal arts for university education: grammar, logic, rhetoric, astronomy, geometry, arithmetic, and music.

Completing the study of the seven liberal arts qualified one for further studies in the professions of the time—philosophy, theology, law, and medicine. Though the common knowledge goals of higher education evolved over the centuries, versions of a core liberal arts approach to education are still in place to this day, in universities around the world. Figure 3.1 presents Columbia University's contemporary core requirements for graduation.

| Course | Semesters Required |
|---|---|
| **Literature Humanities ("Lit Hum")** <br><br> A seminar surveying the great works of Western literature | 2 |
| **Contemporary Civilization** <br><br> A seminar surveying the great works of Western philosophy and social theory | 2 |
| **Art Humanities ("Art Hum")** <br><br> A seminar surveying the great works of Western art | 1 |
| **Music Humanities ("Music Hum")** <br><br> A seminar surveying the great works of Western music. | 1 |
| **University Writing** <br><br> A seminar designed to inculcate university-level writing skills | 1 |
| **Foreign Language** <br><br> A distribution requirement to instill at least an intermediate level of a foreign language | 4 |
| **Frontiers of Science** <br><br> A lecture and seminar course designed to instill "scientific habits of mind" | 1 |
| **Other Science** <br><br> A distribution requirement over any scientific disciplines | 2 |
| **Global Core** <br><br> A distribution requirement to lessen the Eurocentric biases of the other Core classes | 2 |
| **Physical Education** | 2 |

Figure 3.1 Columbia University's Core Requirements
*Source:* Columbia University

Knowledge discipline standards in secondary education in the United States were first established in 1893 by the Committee of Ten, led by Charles Eliot, the president of Harvard University and sponsored by the National Education Association. He convened ten committees of education experts, led mostly by college presidents and deans, and charged them with defining the standardized curriculum requirements for all public secondary schools.

To various degrees, these early education discipline standards (minus the Greek, Latin, and other specific language requirements) are still reflected in secondary school graduation requirements in many education systems today. Figure 3.2 shows a summary of the work of the Committee of Ten (*p.* refers to the number of class periods required).

Table III of the Report of the Committee of Ten

| 1st Secondary School Year. | 2nd Secondary School Year. |
|---|---|
| Latin ..................... 5 p. | Latin .................... 4 p. |
| English Literature, 2 p.⎱ .. 4 p. | Greek .................... 5 p. |
| " Composition, 2 p.⎰ | English Literature, 2 p.⎱ .. 4 p. |
| German [or French] ........ 5 p. | " Composition, 2 p.⎰ |
| Algebra ................... 4 p. | German, continued ........ 4 p. |
| History of Italy, Spain, and | French, begun ............ 5 p. |
| France ................. 3 p. | Algebra,* 2 p.⎱ ........ 4 p. |
| Applied Geography (European | Geometry, 2 p.⎰ |
| political — continental and | Botany or Zoölogy ........ 4 p. |
| oceanic flora and fauna) .. 4 p. | English History to 1688 ..... 3 p. |
| ‾‾‾‾‾ 25 p. | ‾‾‾‾‾ 33 p. |
| | * Option of book-keeping and commercial arithmetic. |

| 3rd Secondary School Year. | 4th Secondary School Year. |
|---|---|
| Latin ..................... 4 p. | Latin .................... 4 p. |
| Greek .................... 4 p. | Greek .................... 4 p. |
| English Literature. 2 p.⎱ | English Literature, 2 p.⎱ |
| " Composition, 1 p.⎰ .. 4 p. | " Composition, 1 p.⎰ .. 4 p. |
| Rhetoric, 1 p.⎰ | " Grammar, 1 p.⎰ |
| German ................... 4 p. | German ................... 4 p. |
| French ................... 4 p. | French ................... 4 p. |
| Algebra,* 2 p.⎱ ........ 4 p. | Trigonometry, ⎱ ......... 2 p. |
| Geometry, 2 p.⎰ | Higher Algebra. ⎰ |
| Physics .................. 4 p. | Chemistry ................ 4 p. |
| History, English and | History (intensive) and Civil |
| American ............... 3 p. | Government ........... 3 p. |
| Astronomy, 3 p. 1st ½ yr.⎱ 3 p. | Geology or Physiography, ⎱ |
| Meteorology, 3 p. 2nd ½ yr.⎰ | 4 p. 1st ½ yr. ⎰ .. 4 p. |
| ‾‾‾‾‾ 34 p. | Anatomy, Physiology, and ⎰ |
| * Option of book-keeping and commercial arithmetic. | Hygiene, 4 p. 2nd ½ yr. ⎰ |
| | ‾‾‾‾‾ 33 p. |

Figure 3.2 Required Courses
*Source:* Committee of Ten Report

The evolution of encyclopedias and the birth of modern library science have also contributed to the organization of the knowledge disciplines, such as the high-level knowledge schemes outlined in Table 3.1.

| Pliny the Elder's Encyclopedia, A.D. 79 | Francis Bacon's Encyclopedia, 1620 | Encyclopedia Britannica, 1971 | Dewey Decimal System, 1876 | Library of Congress System, 1897 |
|---|---|---|---|---|
| Natural History | Nature | Matter & Energy | Gen. Works, Comp Sci | General Works |
| Architecture | Man | The Earth | Philosophy & Psychology | Philosophy, Psychology, Religion |
| Medicine | Man's Action on Nature | Life | Religion | Sciences of History |
| Geography | | Human Life | Social Sciences | World History |
| Geology | | Society | Language | American History |
| | | Art | Pure Science | Other Country Histories |
| | | Technology | Technology | Geography, Anthropology, Recreation |
| | | Religion | Arts & Recreation | Social Science |
| | | History | Literature | Political Science |
| | | Branches of Knowledge | History & Geography | Law |
| | | | | Education |
| | | | | Music |
| | | | | Fine Arts |
| | | | | Language & Literature |
| | | | | Science |
| | | | | Medicine |
| | | | | Agriculture |
| | | | | Technology |
| | | | | Military Science |
| | | | | Naval Science |
| | | | | Library Science |

Table 3.1 Knowledge Classifications
*Source:* CCR

With the arrival of the Information Age, both the amount of new knowledge produced, and the ease of accessing this knowledge, expanded exponentially. New and more innovative knowledge maps are now needed to help us navigate the complexities of our expanding landscape of knowledge.

A wide variety of new knowledge representations are now possible using new technologies such as Big Data, cloud computing, artificial intelligence, and visualization techniques. The areas of knowledge mapping and the dynamic display of information are producing amazing new visualizations, such as this snapshot of a simulation showing the dynamic relationships among scientific fields based on the number of cross-referenced clicks across scientific papers (see Figure 3.3).

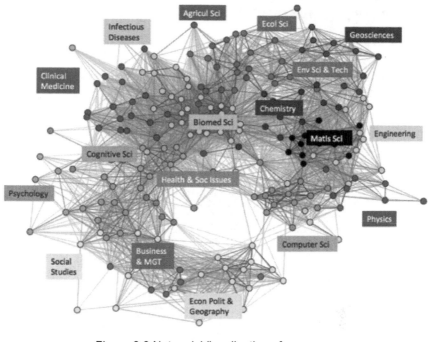

Figure 3.3 Network Visualization of
Science-Related Disciplines
Source: Ismael Rafols, Alan L. Porter, and Loet Leydesdorff, "Science
Overlay Maps: A New Tool for Research Policy and Library
Management," Journal of the American Society for Information Science
and Technology 61, no. 9 (2010): 1871–1887.

CCR will endeavor over the next several years to produce
knowledge maps that help explain the relationship within and
between disciplines, as part of an effort to redesign knowledge
standards from the ground up. Understanding the interrelatedness
of knowledge areas will help to uncover a logical and effective
progression for learning that achieves deep understanding.

Highlighting and following connections among knowledge
domains is in line with research on the development of expertise
and the cognitive underpinnings of understanding, which point to
the importance of the networks of connections between concepts in
students' minds.

# Curating Traditional Disciplines for Relevance

The traditional disciplines taught in most education systems around the world are:

- Maths

- Science

- Languages—domestic

- Languages—foreign

- Social Studies (history, geography, civics, economics, etc.)

- Arts (including music)

- Wellness (often physical education in particular)

In many curricula these disciplines take up most of the available time, and leave little space for newer subjects and topics within the discipline itself, modern disciplines, skills, character development, or meta-learning (discussed in Chapter 6, "The Meta-Learning Dimension"). This leads to student and teacher frustration, as the needs of individuals and societies are generally well understood to require more than traditional knowledge, even without exhaustive justification. Yet without a deep redesign of the standards and corresponding assessments, the situation has not changed significantly over the past decades. Instead of trimming, curating, and redesigning the curriculum, we have continued to overburden it.

This traditional system also tends to encourage the quantity of (testable) knowledge, rather than the depth of understanding and ability to use knowledge with competencies (skills, character, and meta-learning). What if the larger education system was aligned with the goals of personal fulfillment and societal progress, including employability? To get there, we'll have to make difficult choices about what is most relevant for the twenty-first century, and what is not.

So how does one rethink what matters in the traditional disciplines while remaining rigorous and adding flexibility? How does one factor in the instant availability of factual and procedural knowledge on the Internet? How does one *carefully* pare back pieces that are less relevant, to make room for the learning of modern knowledge areas and competencies required for the twenty-first century? The answer lies in examining four ways of slicing any given discipline in order to identify its essential components. This line of thought is illustrated briefly below, with mathematics as the core example.

### 1. Concepts and Meta-Concepts[38]

What are the ideas that students will carry with them throughout their lives, either due to direct practical value or enrichment of worldview? What is essential to a given discipline? What are the concepts that stick long after students have graduated school?

One example of a concept from mathematics may be rate of change. Many students learn this idea first as slope, memorize its definition as rise over run, and learn to find it if given certain information about a line. Rate of change gains deeper significance when applied to physics, in considering the relationship between position, velocity, and acceleration. Since each one is the rate of change of the one before, one can see how these constructs relate to each other. Of course, this idea is ubiquitous in the sciences, but the abstract form of the concept can be useful even to students who do not go on to a STEM field, and use only a

---

[38] CCR, http://curriculumredesign.org/wp-content/uploads/Maths-Concepts-Processes-CCR.pdf

minimal amount of math in their daily lives. It is important because it is a rigorous way to think about change, and change is everywhere in the world. Even non-epidemiologists need to understand rate of change when considering the spread of a disease like Ebola, in order to make decisions about their personal health and safety. An excellent example of a curated set of essential concepts was developed by the American Association for the Advancement of Science through its Project 2061 work, which highlights, by age group, which science concepts should be mastered.[39]

Meta-concepts are concepts that are inherently overarching across the discipline and sometimes beyond, to other disciplines, rather than limited to a given subject itself.

In mathematics, one such meta-concept is proof. The idea of robust proof is of course applicable across mathematics, but also beyond mathematics. For example in philosophy, students must learn to create an argument where each piece builds on the piece before, and to dissect others' arguments critically, looking for leaps of logic and unfounded assertions. This reasoning can be applied to dissecting arguments made in the public sphere, from marketing claims to political rhetoric.

---

[39] American Association for the Advancement of Science, Project 2061, http://www.aaas.org/report/science-all-americans

## 2. Processes, Methods, and Tools[40]

Processes are the big picture elements of every discipline, and will vary widely from field to field. For mathematics, the processes may be:[41] formulating questions mathematically; employing mathematical concepts, facts, procedures, and reasoning; and interpreting outcomes and conclusions.

Processes can then be divided further into methods. These refer to reasoning skills within a given discipline. In mathematics, one such method is called divide and conquer: you learn to break a difficult problem into pieces, and solve the pieces separately. This method is essential for many real-life challenges from all disciplines and careers. For example, if one wants to write a book, one might create an outline, and then tackle each piece separately, before putting it all together into a cohesive piece of writing. Lastly, tools correspond to the most granular types of methods, such as the use of multiplication tables.

## 3. Branches, Subjects, and Topics[42]

Branches, subjects, and topics are the traditional ways of slicing disciplines. Within this slicing, there are some that are more and less relevant to the changing world. Which are the ones that matter

---

[40] CCR, *Mathematics for the 21st Century: What Should Students Learn?*, *Paper 2, Methods and Tools*, http://curriculumredesign.org/wp-content/uploads/Maths-Methods-Tools-CCR.pdf

[41] OECD, *Pisa 2015: Draft Mathematics Framework*, www.oecd.org/pisa/pisaproducts/Draft%20PISA%202015%20Mathematics%20Framework%20.pdf

[42] CCR, http://curriculumredesign.org/wp-content/uploads/Maths-Branches-Subjects-and-Topics-CCR1.pdf

increasingly? In mathematics, relevant new branches could be "discrete mathematics," with subjects such as game theory, and topics such as "the Prisoner's Dilemma." These topics may relate to a wide variety of issues facing individuals and society. For example, doping in sports is a Prisoner's Dilemma, because two competing athletes are better off if neither takes enhancement drugs, but if one takes it, then the other loses. Another example is in economics: Advertising costs companies money, yet if they do not advertise while other companies do, they lose clients.

### 4. How Can We Make Constructs More Interdisciplinary?

Because knowledge can transfer beyond disciplines, it is natural to consider the ways that connections with other knowledge areas can be made explicit. Highlighting interdisciplinary applications of concepts, meta-concepts, methods, and tools can be a powerful way of illustrating concepts and making them immediately relevant to students. For instance, exponentials (from mathematics) can be taught alongside compound interest (from finance) and financial bubbles (history, sociology), as well as bacteria growth (biology) and resource exhaustion (environmental literacy).

It might seem that such a re-organization is impossible. Some may argue that the reason for our current knowledge structure in education is that many concepts are so complex that in order to teach them effectively they must first be broken down into manageable chunks. Over time, they say, the deeper patterns emerge, but only once the student has understood the component pieces. One cannot really learn to understand an ecosystem without first understanding what biotic and abiotic components are, and the different levels of the food chain, from primary producers and primary consumers to secondary consumers, tertiary consumers, quaternary consumers, and decomposers.

But in fact, these vocabulary words will not be useful to students outside of their biology class unless they go on to study biology professionally, in which case they will relearn them anyway. This tends to be true for many jobs—on the job training covers a large portion of what someone needs to know to be successful in that role. We will never be able to know all of the specifics of a given subject, especially because our understanding will continue to change. And we have instant access to any up-to-date information we want, via the internet. Clearly, learning as much of the specifics as possible should not be the goal of teaching a particular subject in school. And there is another problem: such concepts often are not taught their own intrinsic value but rather are taught for their instrumental value toward some later concept or topic, and students have a hard time engaging with and retaining this knowledge.

So what will stick for the students who engaged meaningfully with the material and learned from it but did not go on to become biologists? Perhaps it is the way that organisms self-organize into hierarchies and networks of competition and cooperation, which all use the sun's energy passed through different organisms, or the implications that this has for how we as humans interact with the environment. (CCR will work with experts in each field to determine what these aspects are in the coming years). While traditional structure does include these concepts, they are often hidden in conclusions behind paragraphs and even chapters describing the specifics, and students often feel overwhelmed with the amount of content to learn. Reshaping the learning goals from a focus on covering all of the content in a particular subject or topic, to understanding the key aspects in a meaningful way will improve comprehension, retention, and the learning experience of students.

Because each lesson has intrinsic value, and is not largely taught because it is necessary for the next lesson or for a class in college, students can engage with the material and internalize it, instead of trying to motivate themselves with the promise of its instrumental value. All students, no matter what they later choose to specialize in, have the foundational elements that enable them to intelligently engage with specialists, by grounding their thinking in the concepts and processes central to each discipline.

At this stage, one might also ask: why not regroup traditional knowledge differently, not along disciplines but along big ideas and the like? The answer is, in one word, feasibility. All around the world, teaching is segmented along the lines of disciplines, and although we advocate for a crisp rethinking of what is taught, its interdisciplinarity, and so on, we are also conscious that wholesale abandonment of disciplines is implausibly complex to achieve realistically, at this stage.[43] It is clearly worthy of further explorations so that over time, some shifts may occur, assisted by an increased focus on competencies. Only through a significant bottom-up redesign taking into account all the questions posed above will we be able to cogently adjust the essentials of what one must learn from traditional disciplines.

## Three Aspects of Value

In addition to the process described above, one needs to keep in mind that each subject area has three aspects of value:

- Practical—Students need the concepts and meta-concepts and concepts, processes, methods and tools, and branches, subjects, and topics of this subject in their everyday lives, and for many of the projected jobs of the future.

- Cognitive—Studying a subject enhances higher level thinking such as critical thinking, creativity, and character development, and these skills transfer to other subjects and contexts.

---

[43] Finland is starting a partial migration to topics:
www.oph.fi/english/education_development/current_reforms/curriculum_reform_2016

• Emotional—A subject area has inherent beauty and power to help understand the world, so its deep beauty should be communicated to students because it is one of the great achievements of our species, and this can serve as a source of motivation for students.

For each discipline, these three layers are applicable to various degrees.

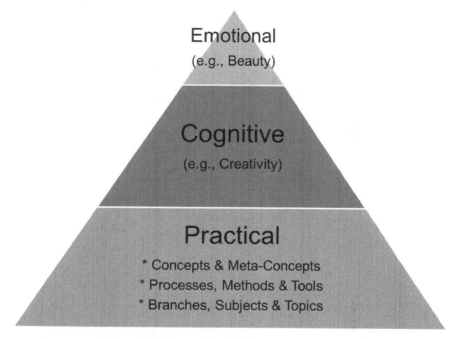

Figure 3.4 Pyramid of Values
Source: CCR

Broadly speaking, the practical aspects of a discipline are the most subject to change as the world continues to change, the essential knowledge base of humanity continues to grow, and the necessary knowledge for jobs continues to change. Something that had great practical value in the past may become outdated, and we must be intentional about carefully considering the practical importance of the subjects we teach.

Whether a subject has cognitive benefits beyond its practical uses is an empirical question that should be explored and tested in the learning sciences. Although we may believe that certain subjects lend themselves to deeper transfer effects, these assumptions must be rigorously tested and we must act based on evidence, not traditions or individual stories.

Finally, the emotional dimension of the inherent beauty of a discipline will be to some degree particular to each individual. However, we must be careful to avoid the idea that beauty of a discipline can only be taught once the practical and cognitive aspects have been covered. Beauty is often in a large part responsible for one's intrinsic motivation to pursue a topic. All three aspects can be learned simultaneously.

Carefully examining each discipline along these aspects is an ongoing process of the CCR, so this discussion is in no way meant to reflect a finished product.

# Modern (Interdisciplinary) Knowledge

Surveying the current state of educational curricula around the globe, and considering the new demands of our times, it becomes increasingly clear that a major update to our knowledge goals are long overdue. New, modern interdisciplinary subjects, branches, and topics, focused on essential concepts, meta-concepts, methods, and tools with cross cutting themes[44] need to be included in students' education to equip them with the knowledge necessary for the twenty-first century.

Large transformations are occurring in our world and they require corresponding emphasis on certain topics and themes. These topics and themes may be best taught through certain traditional and modern subjects, branches, and topics. However it is important to note that teaching these subjects does not

---

[44] Themes cut across concepts, meta-concepts, methods, tools, subjects, branches, and topics. They are discussed in more detail in the next section.

automatically prepare students for the changes in the world. There needs to be deliberate emphasis on the relevant learning outcomes for each topic and subject. Below we outline the changes in the world predicted by the Knowledge Forecast 2020,[45] and the associated topics and themes, knowledge areas, and learning outcomes. These tables are not meant to be exhaustive, but serve to illustrate the kinds of curricular redesigns and the kinds of interdisciplinary knowledge that, if done well, will help us meet these new challenges.

*If done well* is an important caveat—many of these modern knowledge areas are already being taught in one way or another in a variety of programs, with varying success. But just learning about human cognitive biases by studying psychology in a traditional, didactic way could lead to very little to change in behavior. Focus on relevant learning goals and effective practices[46] are what will make them stick. These tables are meant as a starting point for further conversation and analysis. The CCR will take on the work of rigorously fleshing out these ideas in its future work.

## Human Lifespan Extension

The average lengthening of the human lifespan will effect large collective changes in the dynamics of societies, including a larger workforce, deeper institutional expertise, more intergenerational interactions, possibly increased resistance to some transformative changes, and greater demands on healthcare and pension systems.

This may also lead to personal and economic impacts such as having many more careers over a person's lifetime, and potential conflicts over resource allocations between younger and older generations. Such developments will require a high level of intergenerational sensitivity, and a heightened community

---

[45] KnowledgeWorks Foundation, Forecast 2020, discussed in Chapter 1, "Exponential Progress" section.
[46] See Chapter 7, "Briefly Touching on the *How*."

mindset—where everyone must strike a comfortable balance between personal and societal needs.

Note: as highlighted above in the *if-done-well* caveat, the learning outcomes featured in this section's tables will also be deepened through the practices described in Chapter 7's "Briefly Touching on the *How*" section.

| Topics & Themes | Knowledge Areas (Traditional & Modern) | Learning Outcomes |
|---|---|---|
| Personal health. | Wellness (Nutrition, Exercise, Sports, Mindfulness, Kinesthetics, etc.). | Self-direction in managing personal wellness, health knowledge, and practices. |
| Career pathways, Employability, literacy. | Financial literacy. Economics. | Financial awareness and responsibility. Career awareness and self-actualization. |

Table 3.2 Human Lifespan Extension
*Source:* CCR

# Connected People, Organizations, and Planet

The rapid increase in the degree to which people in the world are interconnected brings many compounding effects, including exponential increases in the speed at which information and ideas are disseminated, and the scale of human interactions. An idea can now be described, made into a meme, become viral, become a movement, and turn into demonstrations of thousands of people, in the span of just a few days. Thriving in this hyper-connected world will require greater tolerance for cultural diversity, practices, and worldviews, as well as the ability to use this diversity for more creative solutions to our world challenges.

| Topics & Themes (Themes indicated by *) | Knowledge Areas (Traditional & Modern) | Learning Outcomes |
|---|---|---|
| Social skills. Emotional Intelligence. | Psychology. Sociology. Anthropology. Political science. World history. Civics & Global citizenship. Comparative religions. World Music & Theater. | Understanding the thoughts, feelings, perspectives and motivations of others. Collaboration and teamwork both virtually and viscerally across numerous cultural differences. |
| * Global literacy. | Cultural studies. (geography, global history, ethnography, music, etc.). Media/Journalism. Foreign languages & linguistics. International business & economics. | Global perspectives: understanding global events, cultural practices and behaviors in a variety of cultures. |
| * Systems thinking. | Maths (complex systems) Integrated disciplines (i.e., robotics, biosystems, business, etc.). Environmental & ecological studies. Future studies. | Interconnectedness. Causality. Ecological interactions. Forecasting. |

Table 3.3 Connected People
*Source:* CCR

# The Rise of Smart Machines and Systems

The increasing development and spread of smart machines—technologies that can perform cognitively complex tasks once considered only achievable by humans—has led to increased automation of jobs and production of goods. This in turn is creating dramatic changes in the workforce and overall economic instabilities with larger economic gaps in income and employment. At the same time, it pushes us towards overdependence on technology—potentially decreasing our individual resourcefulness and independence.

These shifts have placed an emphasis on technological savvy, and non-automatable skills (such as synthesis, creativity, etc.). They also affect a desire to be less consumptive and more creative, adopting a do-it-yourself (DIY), maker mindset,[47] which creates a more proactive human-technology balance (being in control of what, when, and how to rely on technology).

| Topics & Themes (Themes indicated by *) | Knowledge Areas (Traditional & Modern) | Learning Outcomes |
|---|---|---|
| * Digital Literacy | Computer Science. Programming. Engineering. Robotics. Synthetic Biology. Maker/DIY skills (i.e., 3D printing, laser-cutting). | Computational thinking (logic, recursiveness, etc.). Data collection & analysis. |
| * Design Thinking | Customer surveying. Design and prototyping. Project management. Entrepreneurship. | Critical & creative thinking. Conscientiousness in carrying out all aspects of complicated projects. |
| Synthesis & Integration | Writing (literature, journalism, technical writing). Research. | Ability to define projects, develop plans, carry out complicated processes and evaluate results, and present findings with precision & clarity. |
| Ethical Mindset | Philosophy (Ethics). | Ethical Behavior. Self-Reflection. |

Table 3.4 Smart Machine Topics and Themes
*Source:* CCR

---

[47]Wikipedia, "Maker Culture," https://en.wikipedia.org/wiki/Maker_culture

# Big Data and New Media

The influx of digital technologies and the wide spectrum of opportunities to communicate with new media have increasingly displaced the solitary use of text as the dominant form of communication. Images and videos, once reserved for the few, are now the majority of our communication online. In the future, aspects of virtual reality will be increasingly integrated, and students must be prepared to communicate in new ways in such a world.

The everyday use of big data—online systems that depend on storing vast amounts of information to provide essential services—brings with it tremendous advantages and concerns. Massive data sets generated by millions of individuals afford us the ability to create simulations and models, allowing for deeper understanding of complex social dynamics, patterns, and ultimately, for supporting better evidence-based decision-making. At the same time, such big data collections and practices raise the issues of privacy, security, identity theft, and other potential abuses of personal information.

Harnessing the advantages, while limiting the potential negative outcomes, will require high levels of media literacy, a strong dose of skeptical inquiry by individuals and public agencies, and an eternal watchfulness for potential abuses of ever-increasing collections of our private data.

| Topics & Themes (Themes indicated by *) | Knowledge Areas (Traditional & Modern) | Learning Outcomes |
|---|---|---|
| Big data analysis. | Statistics and probabilities.<br><br>Computer<br><br>Science and Engineering. | Understanding how to use large, complex sets of data for learning and decision making.<br><br>Knowing the differences between human and machine learning. |
| Media literacy. | Cinematography & media production.<br><br>Marketing, advertising & sales. | Convincingly convey a message using media forms.<br><br>Persuasion.<br><br>Self-identity/brand management in the digital space. |
| * Digital literacy. | Information technology. | Deep awareness of one's digital footprints.<br><br>Knowing how to adroitly manipulate digital technologies, while understanding their limitations. |
| * Information Literacy | Psychology.<br><br>Sociology.<br><br>Anthropology.<br><br>World history. | Maintain dynamic disposition.<br><br>Consider cultural lenses.<br><br>Cultivate comfort with competing evidence. |

Table 3.5 Media Literacy Topics and Themes
*Source:* CCR

# Environmental Stresses and Demands

As discussed above, human society is using its environmental resources at unprecedented rates, consuming more and throwing more of it away than ever before. So far our technologies have extracted from nature an extraordinary bounty of food, energy, and other material resources. Scientists calculate that humans use approximately "40% of potential terrestrial [plant] production"[48] for themselves. What is more, we are also mining the remains of plants and animals from hundreds of millions of years ago (in the form of coal and oil) in the relatively short period of a few centuries. Without technology, we would have no chance of supporting a population of one billion people, much less seven billion and climbing.

A continuation of these trends will likely bring increased competition for resources and a variety of resource shortages that will affect daily life. However, this also creates an increased need for research and development of innovations and the development of more environmentally friendly alternative technologies. This will not only test our ability to develop the professional capacity to pursue these innovations, it will also test our collective commitment to change behavior and accept more varied ways to use, reuse, and conserve resources.

Changing demographics and increased immigration requires greater cooperation and sensitivity within and among nations and cultures. Such needs suggest a reframing of what success means beyond a country's gross domestic product (GDP), which narrowly measures national economic output, and an expansion of business models to include collaboration, tolerance of diversity, sustainability, and other measures that better reflect social progress. It also demands that organizations possess an ability to pursue their goals with an ethical approach to societal challenges.

---

[48] Peter M Vitousek, Paul R. Ehrlich, Anne H. Ehrlich, and Pamela A. Matson, "Human Appropriation of the Products of Photosynthesis," *BioScience* (1986): 368–373.

| Topics & Themes (Themes indicated by *) | Knowledge Areas (Traditional & Modern) | Learning Outcomes |
|---|---|---|
| * Systems thinking. | History (webs of human interactions). Math (complex systems). Sociology. Psychology. Anthropology. Geography. Economics. | Sustainability and interconnectedness. Delayed gratification and long-term thinking. Social perspectives. Persuasion based on evidence. Sustainability. |
| * Environmental literacy. | Environmental & ecological studies. | Interconnectedness. Causality. Ecological interactions. |

Table 3.6 Environmental Topics and Themes
*Source:* CCR

# Amplified Humans

Advances in prosthetic, genetic, and pharmacological supports and enhancements are redefining human capabilities while blurring the lines between disabilities and super-abilities. At the same time, increasing innovation in virtual reality may lead to changes in self-perception and sense of agency in the world.

Such dramatic shifts in one's capabilities requires a rethinking of what it means to be human with such cyber-powers, and demands a rebalancing of our identity, mixing real-world sensations and digital-world simulations.

| Topics & Themes (Themes indicated by *) | Knowledge Areas (Traditional & modern) | Learning Outcomes |
|---|---|---|
| Physical grounding via hand & body skills. | Wellness<br><br>Crafts; Gardening; Carpentry; Cooking; Sewing; Maker/DIY; etc. | Physical proficiency and growth mindset in physical tasks. |
| Empathy.<br><br>Collective responsibility. | Raising pets.<br><br>Caring for others.<br><br>Psychology.<br><br>Sociology.<br><br>Anthropology.<br><br>World history, civics/ethics.<br>Comparative religions, Futures studies. | Develop habits of care.<br><br>Apply social science research to understand self and current events towards designing a better future.<br><br>Seeing commonalities among humankind. |
| Mindfulness.<br><br>Metacognition. | Philosophy.<br><br>Ethics/civics.<br><br>Comparative religions.<br><br>Art & personal expression. | Self-awareness.<br><br>Self-regulation.<br><br>Self-fulfillment.<br><br>Self-transcendence.<br><br>Maturity.<br><br>Wisdom. |

Table 3.7 Amplified Humans Topics and Themes
*Source:* CCR

While there are many programs aimed at teaching these new disciplines and inter-disciplines, the biggest challenge is finding time in the curriculum to focus on them. As expressed previously, the traditional disciplines are taking up all of the currently available time, and they are not sufficient to teach all of the competencies needed for the twenty-first century. In order to make space, we must rethink the goals, benefits, and the relevance of our traditional disciplines and remove the sections that are obsolete or less useful to our times.

As the world becomes increasingly connected, complex, and collaborative, it becomes more necessary to approach questions, problems, issues, and challenges in interdisciplinary ways. Learning is also enhanced when students are able to dive deeply into knowledge areas and make connections between ideas, achieving both depth and breadth in their understanding and competencies. According to Harvard's Project Zero researcher Veronica Boix-Mansilla, "Interdisciplinary learning has been linked to critical thinking skills, more sophisticated conceptions of knowledge, learning and inquiry, and heightened learner motivation and engagement."[49] Interdisciplinary learning will also be required of traditional knowledge areas so that they are not viewed as separate from their real-world applications. Robotics, for example, could be used to teach not only mechanical, electrical, and computer engineering, but also the corresponding concepts in physics and mathematics.

The following modern interdisciplinary knowledge areas are the ones we have identified from the tables above as the most widely applicable and deeply relevant to a successful twenty-first century education approach:

- Technology & Engineering—including computer science, in particular, coding, robotics and artificial intelligence.

- Bioengineering—in particular, genome editing, synthetic biology.

- Media—including journalism (digital) and cinema.

- Entrepreneurship and Business development.

- Personal Finance.

- Wellness – both physical and mental.

- Social Systems – sociology, anthropology, etc.

_____

[49] V. B. Mansilla, *Learning to Synthesize: A Cognitive-Epistemological Foundation for Interdisciplinary Learning.* Harvard Graduate School of Education, 2009, www.frinq-fall2012retreat.michael-flower.com/resources/Learning_to_synthesize.pdf

There certainly may be other modern interdisciplinary knowledge areas of significance, for which we welcome your ideas and feedback.

# Themes

In addition to the twenty-first century goals and competencies, modern interdisciplinary areas of knowledge, and the relevant pieces of traditional disciplines, there is another important aspect to the twenty-first century curriculum—themes. Themes represent common strands of learning that run through many of the disciplines—traditional and modern—and which matter to many jurisdictions and cultures. Teachers, students, and curriculum designers will find countless ways to highlight them throughout the essential areas of study. The relevant themes identified by CCR so far are:

## Global Literacy[50]

Our global community continues to grow more interconnected, and it is no longer enough to learn from the perspective of only one country. To be educated for the twenty-first century, every student now needs to learn each subject from a variety of cultural perspectives[51] from around the world. This means for example that world history includes histories from countries all over the world, math class discusses relevant Eastern (Arab, Indian, and Chinese) mathematicians, not just Western ones, and students are prompted to critically examine their cultural biases and perspectives, and develop understanding and acceptance of other viewpoints. Throughout the curriculum, students should

---

[50] Called global competence by other groups. We do not want the themes to be confused with the 12 competencies of the CCR framework.

[51] The Asia Society has been a highly credible champion of global competence: http://asiasociety.org/globalcompetence

learn to see individual issues within the context of their global socio-cultural significance, gain an international awareness, and a deep appreciation of cultural diversity.

## Information Literacy

According to Eric Schmidt, CEO of Google, every two days we create as much information as was created from the dawn of civilization to 2003.[52] The amount of scientific papers grows by seven to nine percent every year (compounded), which equates to a doubling of scientific output roughly every ten years.[53,54]

While it is true that many people know how to search for information on the Internet, it is not clear that they have grasped the more nuanced reasoning skills necessary to critically evaluate and synthesize what they find, especially when we consider the daunting amount of information they must process.

Twenty-First Century Information Literacy Tools (TILT), a program of The People's Science[55], has identified six core skills and sensibilities for interacting with and applying information in real-world contexts. These objectives outline the essential capacities that must be developed in order to responsibly curate, evaluate, and transform an abundance of information into usable knowledge, as shown in Figure 3.5.

---

[52] M.G. Sigler, "Eric Schmidt: Every 2 Days We Create As Much Information As We Did Up To 2003," *TechCrunch*, http://techcrunch.com/2010/08/04/schmidt-data

[53] Richard Van Noorden, "Global scientific output doubles every nine years," *Nature News Blog*, http://blogs.nature.com/news/2014/05/global-scientific-output-doubles-every-nine-years.html

[54] Ronald Bailey,"Half the Facts You Know Are Probably Wrong," *Reason*, October 2, 2012, https://reason.com/archives/2012/10/02/half-of-the-facts-you-know-are-probably

[55] The People's Science, www.thepeoplesscience.org/tilt, developed by Maya Bialik and Stephanie Sasse.

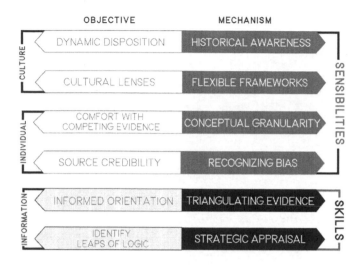

OBJECTIVE          MECHANISM

Figure 3.5 Information Literacy Tools
*Source:* The People's Science

TILT identifies the following core capacities of information literacy:

> • Maintain a dynamic disposition by accepting the progressive nature of information and remaining open to new evidence.
>
> • Consider the role of socio-cultural lenses in the interpretation of information and the proliferation of new ideas.
>
> • Cultivate comfort with competing evidence by acknowledging informed debate as a critical, nuanced step towards replication, refinement, and eventual consensus.
>
> • Evaluate source credibility for common access points in the information dissemination cycle.

• Develop an informed orientation to ensure clarity of how specific evidence is situated in the broader landscape of relevant knowledge.

With information output growing at an unprecedented rate, information literacy skills are increasingly important for all students throughout all subject areas.

# Systems Thinking

Scientific disciplines as well as social systems are converging on the ideas of complex systems (see Figure 3.6).[56] This requires a paradigm shift from the mechanistic and reductionist model of twentieth century Western culture, toward a more balanced approach. Analysis continues to serve a critical purpose by isolating parameters, thereby allowing for their deep treatment and understanding, but it must be integrated with a holistic perspective through synthesis, such that each part can be considered as a whole, each whole as a part of a larger system, and the relationships between all of them explored.[57]

---

[56] Y. Bar-Yam. *Dynamics of Complex Systems*. (Reading, MA: Addison-Wesley, 1997).

[57] Systems thinking is not the same as holistic thinking. It comprises reductionist and holistic thinking together.

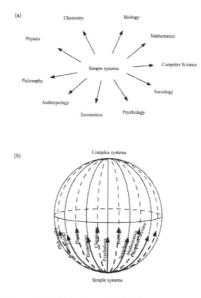

Figure 3.6 Systems Thinking
*Source:* Dynamics of Complex Systems

According to educational theorist and cognitive scientist Derek Cabrera, students should be encouraged to consider distinctions, systems, relationships, and perspectives (DSRP).

- Distinctions: Develop increasingly sophisticated characterizations of ideas and objects.

- Systems: Deconstruct ideas and re-constructing new integrated concepts with a variety of part/whole interactions.

- Relationships: See connections between things.

- Perspectives: See things from different points of view.[58]

---

[58] D. Cabrera et al., "Systems thinking," *Evaluation and Program Planning* 31, no. 3 (2008): 299–310. For a TEDx talk by Dr. Cabrera, see www.youtube.com/watch?v=dUqRTWCdXt4.

By considering the common properties of complex systems, learners can apply this approach to view more traditional disciplines from a modern, systems perspective.

# Design Thinking

As we have seen, the twenty-first century challenges we now face are demanding a major rethinking and redesigning of many of our societal institutions from education, to agriculture and energy use, to product design and manufacturing, to economics and government. Almost every product and service needs to be redesigned in light of our increased use of information and communications technologies, global connectivity, energy and material ecological sustainability, longer lifespans, and increased well-being. Beyond products and services, a design thinking mindset is needed in the ways we approach our challenges.

One way of crisply conceptualizing the design process is through four main principles:[59]

- The human rule: All design activity is ultimately social in nature.

- The ambiguity rule: Design thinkers must preserve ambiguity.

- The redesign rule: All design is redesign (mistakes are a natural part of the process of iterative improvement).

- The tangibility rule: Making ideas tangible facilitates communication.

---

[59] Hasso Plattner, Christoph Meinel, Larry J. Leifer, eds., *Design Thinking: Understand, Improve, Apply. Understanding Innovation* (Berlin; Heidelberg: Springer-Verlag, 2011): xiv–xvi. DOI: 10.1007/978-3-642-13757-0.

An example of a design thinking process model for curriculum is shown in Figure 3.7.

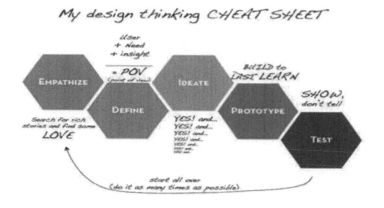

Figure 3.7 Design Thinking
*Source:* Stanford University d:School

# Environmental Literacy

As discussed earlier, humankind is fast approaching or may have surpassed a number of our planet's ecological limits, and to avoid future major environmental crises or ecological disasters, every citizen must have a basic understanding of the fundamentals of environmental science and the impacts of our societies on the long-term sustainability of humankind.

P21 defines the components of environmental literacy as the abilities to:

> • Demonstrate knowledge and understanding of the environment and the circumstances and conditions affecting it, particularly as they relates to air, climate, land, food, energy, water and ecosystems.

> • Demonstrate knowledge and understanding of society's impact on the natural world (e.g., population growth, population development, resource consumption rate, etc.)

• Investigate and analyze environmental issues, and make accurate conclusions about effective solutions.

• Take individual and collective action towards addressing environmental challenges (e.g., participating in global actions, designing solutions that inspire action on environmental issues).

## Digital Literacy

As discussed above, technological savvy is becoming increasingly important. As tools and technologies continue to develop, students must learn to use a variety of new technologies. The majority of jobs are going to require upskilling, as we begin to integrate technological innovations across the majority of possible careers. It is important that students learn to be comfortable with existing technological tools, such as searching on the internet, word processing, spreadsheets, and social media applications, and that they feel comfortable learning new technologies.

All these themes offer educators and students alike a way to make learning more relevant, grounded in the real world, motivating, and action-oriented. They also provide a foundation for interdisciplinary thinking, as they are lenses that educators can mix and match to content areas and competencies.

# The CCR Knowledge Framework Summarized

From the discussion above, we provide the following summary that brings knowledge areas together (see Figure 3.8). As mentioned, this is a work-in-progress and will be further explored as a deep dive into developing the educational goals for each discipline.

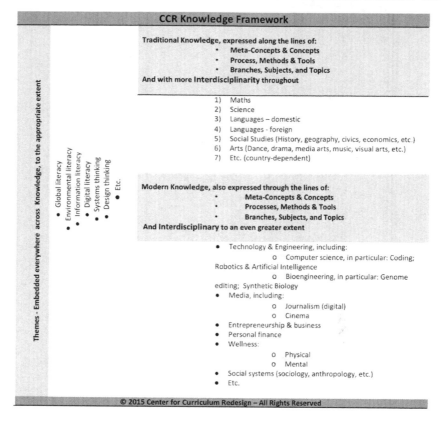

Figure 3.8 CCR Knowledge Framework
*Source:* CCR

# Chapter 4

# The Skills Dimension

Psychological research has shown that active engagement in learning experiences typically leads to better learning outcomes.[60] Instead of just listening, reading, and performing routine exercises, learners exercise their higher level thinking skills by investigating, debating, taking differing viewpoints, and so on. Along with active learning, a constructive approach to learning emphasizes and promotes the social (character) aspects of learning (knowledge is often socially constructed), and the creative skills aspect (knowledge is learned by creating or re-creating it).[61]

In fact, the elusive goal of education transfer—applying what one learns in one setting to another different context—can be thought of as preparation for future learning.[62] This view redefines learning transfer as the productive use of skills and motivations,[63] to prepare students to learn in novel, real-world situations, or in resource-rich environments, that much more closely mirrors learning from real-life challenges. Research has shown that educational environments that emphasize students' active roles, that enhance students' self-regulation, that encourage communication and reflection skills, and are social and relevant to

---

[60] D. Perkins, "Constructivism and Troublesome Knowledge," *in Overcoming Barriers to Student Understanding: Threshold Concepts and Troublesome Knowledge* ed. Jan Meyer et al Ray Land, 33–47 (New York: Routlege, 2006).
[61] D. C. Phillips, "The Good, The Bad, and the Ugly: The Many Faces of Constructivism," *Educational Researcher*, (1995): 5–12.
[62] J. D. Bransford, and D. L. Schwartz, "Rethinking Transfer: A Simple Proposal With Multiple Implications," *Review of Research in Education*, (1999). 61-100.
[63] E. De Corte, "Transfer as the Productive Use of Acquired Knowledge, Skills, and Motivations," *Current Directions in Psychological Science* 12, no. 4, (2003): 142–146.

the learner (character qualities), successfully enhance the transfer of learning to new situations.[64]

# Knowledge and Skills Together

A long-standing debate in education hinges on an assumption that teaching skills will detract from teaching content knowledge. We believe this is another false dichotomy. Studies have shown that when knowledge is learned passively, without engaging skills, it is often only learned at a superficial level (the knowledge may be memorized but not understood, not easily reusable, or short-lived),[65] and therefore not readily transferred to new environments. Deep understanding and application to the real world will occur only by applying skills to content knowledge, so that each enhances the other.

To this end, P21 has created a number of skills maps[66] for several traditional knowledge subject areas: mathematics, science, social studies, geography, English, world languages, and arts.

These skills maps showcase, at different grade levels, the relationships between knowledge and skills and how both can be learned in a mutually reinforcing way. Figure 4.1 is just one example from these skills maps, focusing on the intersections between science knowledge and creativity skills.

---

[64]  Ibid.
[65]  D. Perkins, "Constructivism and Troublesome Knowledge," 33–47.
[66]  P21, Skills Maps, www.p21.org/our-work/resources/for-educators#SkillsMaps

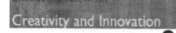

Figure 4.1 Skills Map
*Source:* P21, www.p21.org/storage/documents/twenty-
firstcskillsmap_science.pdf

# Skills and Eduployment Gaps

To respond to the pervasive concern that recent graduates (of secondary school and college/university) lack relevant skills for the workforce, many surveys have been conducted that ask employers to express their views on what their employment needs are. Notable examples include:

• *Are They Really Ready to Work?* by the Conference Board and Partnership for 21st Century Skills.[67]

• *Critical Skills Needs and Resources for the Changing Workforce* by the Society for Human Resource Management and *The Wall Street Journal*.[68]

---

[67] P21, *Are They Ready To Work?*,
www.p21.org/storage/documents/FINAL_REPORT_PDF09-29-06.pdf
[68] Society for Human Resource Management, *Critical Skills Needs and Resources for the Changing Workforce*,

• *OECD Skills Outlook* by the Organization for Economic
Co-operation and Development (OECD).[69]

P21 synthesized all the survey responses and the input of a
wide variety of experts; the results are described in the book *21st
Century Skills: Learning for Life in Our Times.*[70] They are drawn
from a broad global consensus from industry, education and
government, and show consistent convergence on the skills most
needed for learning, productive work, and life success, although
different frameworks often use different terminology and
groupings. Table 4.1 provides a comparison between prominent
skills frameworks.[71]

---

file://localhost/www.shrm.org:research:surveyfindings:articles:documents:critic
al skills needs and resources for the changing workforce survey report.pdf

[69] OECD, *OECD Skills Outlook 2013: First Results from the Survey of Adult
Skills*, OECD Publishing (2013).

[70] Bernie Trilling and Charles Fadel. *21st Century Skills: Learning for Life in
Our Times* (San Francisco, CA: Jossey-Bass/Wiley, 2009).

[71] For more complete crosswalks between the various frameworks, please
consult the CCR website's documents.

| P21.org Skills Framework | ATC21S[1] | OECD Assessment of Adult Competencies (PIACC) | OECD Programme for International Student Assessment (PISA) | Education Ministries, Departments, and Schools feedback to P21 = "focus on 4 C's" for Skills = CCR |
|---|---|---|---|---|
| Learning & Innovation | Ways of thinking | | | |
| Creativity & Innovation | Creativity and innovation | | Creative problem solving | Creativity |
| Critical thinking & Problem solving | Critical thinking Problem solving Decision making | Problem solving | | Critical Thinking |
| | Ways of Working | | | |
| Communication | Communication | Reading (prose and document texts) Writing Oral presentation | | Communication |
| Collaboration | Collaboration (teamwork) | Teamwork | | Collaboration |
| Information, Media & ICT literacy | Tools for Working | | | From here on, these map onto other dimensions of the CCR framework (Knowledge, Character, and Meta-Learning) |
| Information Literacy | Information literacy | Internet use | | |
| Media Literacy | | | | |
| ICT Literacy | ICT literacy | Computer use | | |
| Life & Career Skills | Living in the world Life and career | | | |
| . | | | | |
| Flexibility & Adaptability | | | | |
| Initiative & Self-direction | | Plan own time | | |
| Social & Cross-cultural Skills | Citizenship – local and global Cultural awareness and competence | | | |

[1] Represented in Binkley http://link.springer.com/chapter/10.1007/978-94-007-2324-5_2#page-1

Table 4.1 Comparison of Frameworks and Feedback
*Source:* CCR

Accumulated feedback[72] from policymakers in ministries, departments of education, and schools pointed to a need for more simplicity to make the skills recommendations actionable, hence CCR's focus on the four *C*s: creativity, critical thinking, communication, and collaboration.

The following sections examine each of these 4C skills individually, including its importance and relevant cognitive science and education research. Although we present the skills separately from the knowledge areas they must be applied to for effective learning—all of these skills are to be learned *through* and *with* the learning of content knowledge.

# Creativity

> Imagination is more important than knowledge. For knowledge is limited to all we now know and understand, while imagination embraces the entire world, and all there ever will be to know and understand.
>
> —Albert Einstein

Creativity is traditionally considered to be most directly involved with artistic endeavors such as art and music. While this association has some historical basis, the false equating of creativity exclusively with art is misleading and has been described as art bias.[73]

Recently, creativity has been shown to be integral to a wide range of knowledge and skills, including scientific thinking,[74]

---

[72]   Private communication from Ken Kay, CEO of P21 at the time, with Geoff Garin of Peter Hart Associates (pollster).

[73]   M. A Runco and R. Richards, eds., *Eminent Creativity, Everyday Creativity, and Health.* (Greenwich, CT: Greenwood Publishing Group 1997).

[74]   K. Dunbar, "How Scientists Think: On-Line Creativity and Conceptual Change in Science. Creative Thought: An Investigation of Conceptual Structures and Processes," in T.B. Ward, S.M. Smith and J. Vaid, eds., *Conceptual Structures and Processes: Emergence, Discovery , and Change* (Washington D.C: American Psychological Association Press, 1997).

entrepreneurship,[75] design thinking,[76] and mathematics.[77] A 2010 IBM study interviewed over 15,000 CEOs from 60 countries and 33 industries and found that creativity was named the most important leadership quality to meet the challenges of increasing complexity and uncertainty in the world.[78] Creativity is also an extremely fulfilling human activity. According to Mihaly Csikszentmihalyi, "Most of the things that are interesting, important, and human are the results of creativity . . . When we are involved in [creativity], we feel that we are living more fully than during the rest of life."[79]

Countries have begun to focus on reformulating education around creativity (creative problem solving, idea generation, design thinking, etc.) and innovation. In 2008, British secondary-school curricula were revamped to emphasize idea generation and pilot programs have begun measuring their progress. The European Union designated 2009 as the European Year of Creativity and Innovation, and began holding conferences and funding relevant teacher trainings in problem- and project-based learning methods. China has begun massive education reforms to replace their traditional rote-teaching style with a more problem/project-based learning approach.[80] Japan has begun to implement educational and economic reforms to address their creativity problem.[81]

---

[75] K. K Sarri, I. L. Bakouros, and E. Petridou, "Entrepreneur Training for Creativity and Innovation," *Journal of European Industrial Training* 34, no. 3 (2010): 270–288.

[76] K. Dorst and N.Cross, "Creativity in the Design Process: Co-Evolution of Problem–Solution," *Design Studies* 22, no. 5, (2001): 425–437.

[77] L. J. Sheffield, "Creativity and School Mathematics: Some Modest Observations," *Zdm* 45 no. 2 (2013): 325–332.

[78] IBM, *Capitalizing on Complexity: Insights from the Global Chief Executive Officer Study*, 2010, http://public.dhe.ibm.com/common/ssi/ecm/gb/en/gbe03297usen/GBE03297US EN.PDF

[79] Mihaly Csikszentmihalyi, . *Creativity: Flow And The Psychology Of Discovery And Invention* (New York: HarperCollins, 1997)

[80] P. Bronson, Merryman, "The Creativity Crisis." *Newsweek*, 2010, www.newsweek.com/creativity-crisis-74665

[81] Amy McCreedy, "The 'Creativity Problem' and the Future of the Japanese Workforce," *Asia Program Special Report* 121 (2004): 1–3.

The dominant creativity model in the research literature defines creative individuals as possessing divergent-thinking abilities, including idea production, fluency, flexibility, and originality.[82] The sketches in Figure 4.2[83] illustrate each of these qualities and how they relate to sample answers on a test of students' creativity.

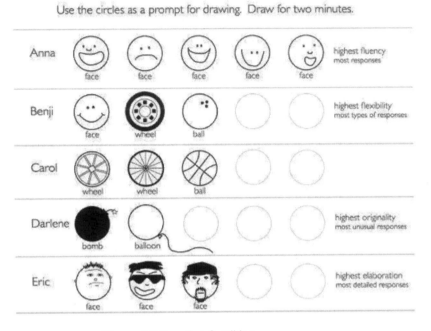

Figure 4.2 Creative Qualities
*Source:* Peter Nilsson,
www.senseandsensation.com/2012/03/assessing-creativity.html

This model of creativity has inspired diverse divergent thinking exercises and tests designed to enhance and measure creativity. While there has been some controversy in the literature,

---

[82]   J. P Guilford, *Intelligence, Creativity, and Their Educational Implications* (San Diego, CA: Robert R. Knapp, 1968).
[83]   Peter Nilsson, "Four Ways to Measure Creativity," *Sense and Sensation Writing on Education, Creativity, and Cognitive Science*, 2012, www.senseandsensation.com/2012/03/assessing-creativity.html

a large meta-analysis[84] has found that divergent thinking tasks on tests predict creative achievement more accurately than IQ, although they are correlated to some degree.

Broadly speaking, teaching for creativity is complementary with teaching for content knowledge. Open-ended, problem-based learning is more likely to encourage students to think creatively than paper and pencil exercises in which there is only one right answer. Prompting people to think in a humorous way has also been found to increase creativity, as it cues the brain to think in ways that are not necessarily tied to reality.[85] Play in general is uniquely suited to enhance creative thinking.[86]

When teaching for creativity it is important to remember that creative thinking can take place at various levels. Figure 4.3 organizes activities according to the creativity involved: from perfect imitation (involving no novelty), to the elusive idea of complete originality (with a high degree of novelty in both form and content). Table 4.2 shows how there are opportunities for creativity in the classroom across all of these levels.

---

[84] K. H. Kim, "Meta-Analyses of the Relationship of Creative Achievement to Both IQ and Divergent Thinking Test Scores," *The Journal of Creative Behavior* 42 no. 2 (2008): 106–130.

[85] A. Ziv, "The Influence of Humorous Atmosphere on Divergent Thinking," *Contemporary Educational Psychology* 8, no. 1 (1983): 68–75.

[86] S. W. Russ, "Play, Creativity, and Adaptive Functioning: Implications for Play Interventions," *Journal of Clinical Child Psychology* 27, no. 4 (1998): 469–480.

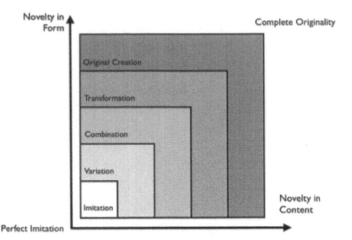

Figure 4.3 Creativity in the Classroom
*Source:* Peter Nilsson,
www.senseandsensation.com/2012/03/taxonomy-of-creative-design.html

| Level of Creativity | Definition | Classroom Example |
|---|---|---|
| Imitation | Creation by identical replication. This is a foundational skill, and is often the starting point for more creative tasks. | Memorize an excerpt of a piece of literature and perform it aloud in class. |
| Variation | Creation by varying a particular aspect or aspects of the work, and imitating the rest exactly. | Rewrite a sentence from a piece of literature with the same grammatical structure, by changing the subject matter and vocabulary. |
| Combination | Mixture of two or more works into one, new work. | Create a Rube Goldberg machine out of the simple machines learned in class. |
| Transformation | Translation of an existing work into a different medium or representation. | Create a timeline of historical events based on class notes that separates political, social, and economic threads. |
| Original Creation | Creation of a new piece of work that is only very distantly, if at all, related to previous works. | Write a short story. |

Table 4.2 Classroom Examples of Creativity
*Source:* CCR, adapted from Peter Nilsson

Although more open-ended assignments demand greater creativity, they are not necessarily more effective in teaching creativity. If students have not built up the necessary skills, assignments that are too open-ended will be overwhelming and ineffective. Teachers should set helpful boundaries within which to innovate, according to the learning outcomes they hope to accomplish. Having strong constraints around a challenge can also increase the need for even more creative approaches.

Creativity may well be the most important skill for students to learn for the twenty-first century, as it is necessary for devising innovative solutions to the many twenty-first century challenges we face.

# Critical Thinking

> Education must enable one to sift and weigh evidence, to discern the true from the false, the real from the unreal, and the facts from the fiction. The function of education, therefore, is to teach one to think intensively and to think critically.
>
> —Martin Luther King, Jr.

The National Council for Excellence in Critical Thinking defines critical thinking as the "intellectually disciplined process of actively and skillfully conceptualizing, applying, analyzing, synthesizing, and/or evaluating information gathered from, or generated by, observation, experience, reflection, reasoning, or communication, as a guide to belief and action."[87]

Although this encompasses a wide range of mental activities such as problem solving, decision making, researching, effective reasoning, systems thinking, and critiquing, in essence, the critical part of critical thinking refers to questioning claims, rather than accepting them at face value. Historian William Graham Sumner defines critical thinking as:

> the examination and test of propositions of
> any kind which are offered for acceptance,

---

[87] National Council for Excellence in Critical Thinking, "Defining Critical Thinking," www.criticalthinking.org/pages/defining-critical-thinking/766

in order to find out whether they correspond
to reality or not. The critical faculty is a
product of education and training. It is a
mental habit and power. It is a prime
condition of human welfare that men and
women should be trained in it. It is our only
guarantee against delusion, deception,
superstition, and misapprehension of
ourselves and our earthly circumstances.[88]

Critical thinking in education can be traced back to the work of Socrates, who used questions to encourage his students to clarify their assumptions and back up their claims, pushing past ideas that seemed self-evident and exposing the underlying biases and gaps in reasoning. Now, over 2,400 years later, critical thinking remains a top priority for education. Such habits of mind that comprise critical thinking have been "consistently and emphatically identified by those who teach entry-level college courses as being as important or more important than any specific content knowledge taught in high school."[89]

And yet, in part because they are more challenging to assess, critical thinking skills have been too often absent from curricula overburdened with facts and procedures. Instead, students often learn how to take tests, a skill that is rarely transferrable beyond the education system. Textbooks also play a role, by breaking down complex problems into parts that are so manageable that students perform them without engaging in much meaningful critical thinking.

The most famous characterization of the components of critical thinking comes from Bloom's Taxonomy of Educational Objectives. Since then, many have taken similar components and organized or described them differently. Figure 4.5 is a comparison

---

[88]  W. G. Sumner, *Folkways: A Study of the Sociological Importance of Usages, Manners, Customs, Mores, and Morals* (New York: Ginn and Co., 1940): 632, 633.
[89]  D. Conley, *Toward A More Comprehensive Conception of College Readiness* (Eugene, OR: Educational Policy Improvement Center, 2007).

of the taxonomies, all illustrating educational goals in some progression from lower levels of knowledge access (retrieval, remembering, etc.) to higher levels of understanding and use (analysis, synthesis, evaluation, etc.).

| Taxonomies of Educational Objectives | | | |
|---|---|---|---|
| Bloom (1956) | Anderson & Krathwohl (2001) | Marzano & Kendall (2006) | PISA (2000) |
| Evaluation | Create | Self-System Thinking | Communicate |
| Synthesis | Evaluate | Metacognition | Construct |
| Analysis | Analyze | Knowledge Utilization | Evaluate |
| Application | Apply | Analysis | Integrate |
| Comprehension | Understand | Comprehension | Manage |
| Knowledge | Remember | Retrieval | Access |

Figure 4.4 Taxonomies of Educational Objectives
*Source*: L.M. Greenstein, *Assessing Twenty-First Century Skills*

Current learning research indicates that all these levels can be effectively mixed together in learning activities and are not nearly as sequential as Bloom originally thought of them.[90]

Teaching critical thinking can come in many different forms, from an explicit curriculum devoted to identifying and practicing the necessary component critical skills, to projects that involve interpreting information, analyzing parts and wholes, analysis and synthesis, evaluating evidence, taking multiple perspectives, discerning patterns, and grasping abstract ideas.[91] Teaching critical thinking is often tied closely to developing reflective or metacognitive habits of mind, as each can support and strengthen the other.[92] The main challenge is the successful transfer of critical thinking skills to contexts outside the one in which they were learned.

---

[90] From: L.W. Anderson and D. R. Krathwohl, eds. et al., *A Taxonomy for Learning, Teaching, and Assessing: A Revision of Bloom's Taxonomy of Educational Objectives,* (New York: Longman, 2001).

[91] L. M. Greenstein, *Assessing Twenty-First Century Skills: A Guide To Evaluating Mastery And Authentic Learning* (Thousand Oaks, CA: Corwin Press, 2012).

[92] D. Kuhn, "A Developmental Model of Critical Thinking," *Educational Researcher* 28, no. 2 (1999): 16–46.

# Communication

Although only some professions are based on communication at their core (such as news reporting, therapy, public speaking, and teaching), all professions require various forms of it on a regular basis (negotiating, giving instructions, advising, building relationships, resolving conflicts, etc.).[93] In fact, the explicit teaching of communication is explored in research contexts from preschool to medical school.[94]

Traditional classwork, such as writing papers and giving presentations, is often one-sided, and thus not truly interactive communication. It is often inconsequential whether or not the intended audience (other than the teacher) successfully understands the message. It may not effectively achieve the various components of critical thinking, such as active listening, clear thinking and writing, and persuasive presenting. For this reason, collaborative tasks (discussed in the collaboration skills section below) can be an important way to learn, measure, and get important feedback on the growth of true communication skills.

Another method to build authentic communication skills is through peer tutoring—in which students tutor their classmates or younger students. Not only is teaching others a powerful way to enhance communication skills, it provides the immediate feedback of whether the tutored student really understood the material, and thus, whether the communication was successful. This challenge of communication to another student also increases the tutor's

---

[93]  V. S. DiSalvo and J. K. Larsen, "A Contingency Approach to Communication Skill Importance: The Impact of Occupation, Direction, and Position," *Journal of Business Communication* 24, no. 3 (1987): 3–22.
[94]  E. R. Morgan and R. J. Winter, "Teaching Communication Skills: An Essential Part of Residency Training," *Archives of Pediatric Adolescent Medicine* 150 (1996).

effort,[95] and the responsibility of the role increases their self-concept.[96]

In today's digital age, communication skills have become both more important and much more varied. Scholars have noted that adding a focus on media literacy to the traditional reading and writing literacy goals has the potential to "(a) increase learning by making the practices of literacy relevant to students' home cultures and ways of knowing, (b) accommodate diverse learning styles and meet the needs of multicultural learners, and (c) develop creativity, self-expression, teamwork, and workplace skills."[97] As we move forward, we can continue to think about communication in a broad and deep way, as a critical set of skills applied to all knowledge areas and competencies.

## Collaboration

In a world of increasing complexity, the best approaches to solving multifaceted problems involve collaboration among people with different skills, backgrounds, and perspectives.[98] When executed well, collaboration enables a group to make better decisions than any one individual would on his own, since it allows for the consideration of multiple viewpoints.[99] On the other hand, if executed poorly, collaborative efforts are subject to groupthink, and become less effective than an individual.[100] Studies probing

---

[95]C. C. Chase et al., "Teachable Agents and the Protégé Effect : Increasing the Effort Towards Learning," *Journal of Science Education Technology* 18, no. 4 (2015): 334–352.

[96] Vany Martins Franca et al., "Peer Tutoring Among Behaviorally Disordered Students: Academic and Social Benefits to Tutor and Tutee," *Education and Treatment of Children* (1990): 109–128.

[97] R. Hobbs and R. Frost, "Measuring the Acquisition of Media-Literacy Skills," *Reading Research Quarterly* 38, no. 3 (2015): 330–355.

[98] C. Miller and Y. Ahmad, "Collaboration and Partnership: An Effective Response to Complexity and Fragmentation or Solution Built on Sand?" *International Journal of Sociology and Social Policy* 20, no. 5/6 (2000): 1–38.

[99] J. Surowiecki, *The Wisdom of Crowds* (New York: Anchor Books, 2005).

[100] I. L. Janis, "Groupthink," *Psychology Today 5,* no. 6 (1971): 43–46.

the structure of scientific fields have revealed that while there is specialization, interdisciplinary work is often integral to important advancements in knowledge and technology.[101]

Simply put, collaboration is the joining together of multiple individuals in service of working toward a common goal.[102] Several tactics have been proven effective in teaching the skills of collaboration in the classroom:

> 1. Establishing group agreements and accountability for assigned tasks sets the stage for division of labor and synergy of efforts.

> 2. Teaching listening skills allows for the creation of a space where ideas can be shared, received, and applied.

> 3. Teaching the art of asking good questions— particularly, open-ended and thought-provoking ones—facilitates expansion of knowledge and aids progress towards better solutions.

> 4. Practicing and demonstrating the skills of negotiation—patient listening, flexibility, articulating points of agreement, and maintaining the ability to think clearly under pressure—is helpful in any richly collaborative situation.[103]

Collaborative learning has been shown to increase learning outcomes, enjoyment of the subject matter, self-esteem, and inclusiveness of diversity.[104] There are many different pedagogical

---

[101] E. Leahey and R .Reikowsky, "Research Specialization and Collaboration Patterns in Sociology," *Social Studies of Science* 38, no. 3 (2008): 425–440.
[102] Wikipedia, "Collaboration," http://en.wikipedia.org/wiki/Collaboration
[103] R. Alber, "Deeper Learning: A Collaborative Classroom is Key," *Edutopia*, 2012, www.edutopia.org/blog/deeper-learning-collaboration-key-rebecca-alber
[104] R. T. Johnson and D. W. Johnson, "Cooperative Learning in the Science Classroom," *Science and Children* 24 (1986): 31–32.

tools that utilize collaborative learning. Across a meta-analysis, they have been found to be more effective in producing academic achievement than individual or competitive learning.[105] Students are also more positive about school, subject areas, and teachers, as well as each other when they learn collaboratively.[106] Collaboration is also synergistic with the other skills discussed here, serving as an authentic goal of communication (discussed above), and enhancing critical thinking[107] and creativity.[108]

# Applied Learning

Skills represent how we use what we know. The 4C skills outlined above are in high demand by employers, are key to helping students achieve deep understanding of knowledge, and are essential to facilitate the transfer of learning to new environments. These skills are inseparably connected to content knowledge, as it is implausible to teach skills independent of a content knowledge base—e.g., it is impossible to think critically about nothing.

The CCR wholeheartedly supports the notion of knowledge *and* skills developed together in a virtuous cycle, such that the knowledge we engage in our classes becomes the source of creativity, the subject of critical thought and communication, and the impetus for collaboration. In this way, we can better engage in

---

[105] D. W. Johnson, R. T. Johnson, and M. B. Stanne, "Cooperative Learning Methods: A Meta-Analysis," (2000), www.researchgate.net/profile/David_Johnson50/publication/220040324_Cooperative_Learning_Methods_a_Meta-analysis/links/00b4952b39d258145c000000.pdf

[106] D. W. Johnson and R. T. Johnson, "Cooperative Learning and Achievement," In S. Sharan (ed.), *Cooperative Learning* (San Juan Capistrano, CA: Kagan Cooperative Learning, 1990).

[107] A. A. Gokhale, "Collaborative Learning Enhances Critical Thinking," *Journal of Technology Education* 7, no. 1 (1995): 22–25.

[108] B. Uzzi, "Collaboration and Creativity: The Small World Problem," *American Journal of Sociology* 111, no. 2 (2005): 447–504.

the global challenges of today, the new demands of tomorrow's workforce, and the timeless challenges of personal and societal fulfillment in a swiftly changing world.

# Chapter 5

# The Character Dimension

> We have evolved traits that will lead to humanity's extinction—so we must learn how to overcome them.
>
> —Christian de Duve

# Why Develop Character Qualities?

Since ancient times, the goal of education has been to cultivate confident and compassionate students who become successful learners, contribute to their communities, and serve society as ethical citizens. Character education is about the acquisition and strengthening of virtues (qualities), values (beliefs and ideals), and the capacity to make wise choices for a well-rounded life and a thriving society.

Facing the challenges of the twenty-first century requires a deliberate effort to cultivate personal growth and the ability to fulfill social and community responsibilities as global citizens. The Millennium Project tracks 30 variables globally to discern the state of the world[109] and identifies "where we are winning, losing, and unclear/little change."

---

[109] J. C. Glenn, T. J. Gordon, and E. Florescu, "State of the Future," *World Federation of United Nations Associations*, (2007), http://futurestudies.az/pdf/SOF_2008_Eng.pdf

The highly worrisome areas where humanity is losing—environmental issues, corruption, terrorism, income inequality—have significant ethical and character implications (see Figure 5.1).

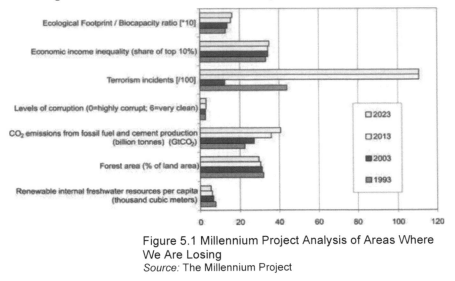

Figure 5.1 Millennium Project Analysis of Areas Where We Are Losing
*Source:* The Millennium Project

At the same time, advances in science and technology present a double-edged sword. Although they provide more opportunities for global collaboration and progress, they also create new ethical challenges such as the use of nuclear energy, pesticides, genetic modification, and more broadly, a paradigm of modern values oriented toward material progress.[110]

Employers around the world also strongly believe in the importance of character education. In a global survey[111] by the Business and Industry Advisory Council (BIAC) to the OECD, 80 percent of representatives of employer organizations from countries as diverse as Austria, Australia, Brazil, Denmark, France, Hungary, Ireland, Italy, Korea, Latvia, Mexico, New Zealand, Sweden, Slovenia, United Kingdom, and the United States,

---

[110] R. Eckersley, "Postmodern Science: The Decline or Liberation of Science?" *Science Communication in Theory and Practice* eds. Susan M. Stocklmayer, Michael M. gore, Chris Bryant, Boston: Kluwer Academic Publishers (2001): 83–94.
[111] Business and Industry Advisory Council, http://biac.org/wp-content/uploads/2015/06/15-06-Synthesis-BIAC-Character-Survey1.pdf

declared that character education is becoming a more important issue, with 100 percent of them responding that their education system should do more to promote character education.

It is through a strong sense of personal and ethical responsibility that students, our citizens of the future, will be better able to make knowledgeable and wise decisions that fully address the great challenges of our times.

# Purposes of Character Education

There are three commonly cited, broad purposes of character education—it can:

- Build a foundation for lifelong learning.

- Support successful relationships at home, in the community, and in the workplace.

- Develop the personal values and virtues for
    sustainable participation in a globalized world.

Our human interdependency is both our strength and weakness. In the words of Nobel Prize winner Christian de Duve: "We have evolved traits [such as group selfishness] that will lead to humanity's extinction—so we must learn how to overcome them."[112] Indeed, our collective well-being is based on our individual awareness. As UNESCO has underscored,[113] "There is every reason to place renewed emphasis on the moral and cultural dimensions of education... this process must begin with self-

---

[112] C. De Duve and N. Patterson, *Genetics Of Original Sin: The Impact Of Natural Selection On The Future Of Humanity* (New Haven, CT: Yale University Press, 2010).
[113] UNESCO, *Learning: The Treasure Within*, 1996, Report from the International Commission on Education in the Twenty-First Century.

understanding through... knowledge, meditation and the practice of self-criticism."

Character development as an educational goal in modern times is sometimes confounded with teaching religion, since the two share a number of similar goals. It is important to note that a religious perspective is not necessary for teaching character qualities. Though religious studies may support character education, it may also add complexity and controversy to character education in today's increasingly pluralistic, secular, and global world. In some countries formal public education and religious development are entirely separate, in others, they are closely linked, with a wide spectrum of variations in between.

Some may argue that teaching children good character qualities should be left to religious leaders and families. However, it is important to realize that schools cannot avoid developing social and ethical values as part of a child's educational development. The values we highlight in this educational dimension are relevant to all humans in the modern world. While family life and out of school activities have often been responsible for this aspect of education, we believe its importance in preparing all students for the challenges they will face in the twenty-first century grants the teaching and learning of character a prominent place in the official curriculum.

Research has shown that students' capacities, beyond academic learning of knowledge and skills, are important predictors of achievement[114] and can be essential to success in work and civic life. While certain knowledge and skills may or may not be used in future jobs, character qualities will invariably be applicable to a wide range of professions and to everyday family and community life.

---

[114] For a review, see Camille A. Farrington et al., *Teaching Adolescents to Become Learners: The Role of Noncognitive Factors in Shaping School Performance—A Critical Literature Review*. Consortium on Chicago School Research. 1313 East 60th Street, Chicago, IL 60637, 2012.

# The Six Character Qualities

> There is every reason to place renewed emphasis on the moral and cultural dimensions of education... this process must begin with self-understanding through... knowledge, meditation and the practice of self-criticism.
> —Report from the International Commission on Education in the Twenty-First Century, UNESCO 1996[115]

First, a quick definition: character encompasses all of the terms: agency, attitudes, behaviors, dispositions, mindsets, personality, temperament, values, beliefs, social and emotional skills, non-cognitive skills, and soft skills.[116] Character, although sometimes charged with non-educational connotations, is a concise and inclusive term that is recognizable by all cultures.

Character qualities—how we behave and engage in the world—are distinct from skills—the ability to effectively use what one knows. Twenty-first century skills (the four Cs of creativity, critical thinking, communication, and collaboration)[117] are essential for acquisition and application of knowledge as well as for work performance and civic life,[118] but knowledge and skills are not entirely sufficient to prepare learners for their future challenges, and character qualities may be much better predictors of student success in further learning, productive work and careers, and active engagement in civic responsibilities.[119]

---

[115] For more information see, www.unesco.org/new/en/education/themes/leading-the-international-agenda/rethinking-education/visions-of-learning

[116] Note that we do not support the incorrect use of the terms non-cognitive skills or soft skills.

[117] Bernie Trilling and Charles Fadel, *21st Century Skills* (San Francisco, CA: Wiley and Sons, 2009).

[118] The Conference Board "Are They Really Ready to Work?" *AMA Critical Skills Survey*, PIAAC program (OECD).

[119] Arthur E. Poropat, "Other-Rated Personality and Academic Performance: Evidence and Implications", *Learning and Individual Differences*,34 (August

Why character qualities? The word "traits" has associations of being fixed and immutable. As we have learned from advances in neuropsychology, our brains are highly plastic or modifiable through learning, and research has shown that many aspects of character qualities can be learned and developed to various degrees.[120] For this reason they are an integral part of the framework for educational goals—because they can and should be achieved and honed through practice. Unlike other similar frameworks such as the "Big 5"[121], we see these qualities as changing throughout a person's life due to exposure and practice; we are interested in cognitive mechanisms, rather than cross-cultural perception of the words used to describe personality.

Since a comprehensive and clear framework fulfilling all of the criteria for actionable educational goals in the character dimension was not found, the CCR synthesized and refined a composite of many frameworks from around the world, including:

| | |
|---|---|
| • Center for the Advancement of Ethics and Character (CAEC) | • Royal Society for the Arts |
| | • Singapore Ministry of Education |
| • Character Counts! Coalition | • South Korea Ministry of Education |
| • CharacterEd.Net | |
| • Character Education Partnership | • Success DNA |
| | • Sweden Ministry of Education |
| • China Ministry of Education | • Thailand Ministry of Education |
| • Facing History and Ourselves | • Young Foundation |
| • KIPP Schools | |
| • Partnership for 21st Century Learning (P21) | |

---

2014): 24–32. See also: Paul Tough, *How Children Succeed: Grit, Curiosity, and the Hidden Power of Character* (New York: Mariner Books, 2013).
[120]T. Lickona, *Character Matters: How to Help Our Children Develop Good Judgment, Integrity, and Other Essential Virtues* (New York: Simon and Schuster, 2004).
[121] Wikipedia, https://en.wikipedia.org/wiki/Big_Five_personality_traits

The CCR's character framework also incorporated the education philosophy of thought leaders such as Howard Gardner,[122] Robert Sternberg,[123] and Edgar Morin,[124] whose key character elements are summarized in Table 5.1.

| Gardner | Sternberg | Morin |
|---|---|---|
| • Disciplined | • Practical | • Pertinence in knowledge |
| • Synthesizing | • Analytical | • Confronting uncertainties |
| • Creating | • Creative | • Detecting errors |
| • Respectful | • Wise | • Understanding each other |
| • Ethical | | • Teaching the human condition |
| | | • Ethics for Humanity |

Table 5.1 Key Elements of Character
Source: CCR

The elements of the character dimension were then iteratively refined with input from more than five hundred teachers from around the world, in late 2014.

Table 5.2 identifies the six essential qualities that emerged from the CCR's research, as well as a host of their closely associated terms.[125] It is important to keep in mind that the list of associated terms is not exhaustive, and the same terms are often used for different qualities, (as well as different terms for the same qualities) in the research literature, making this field ripe for never-ending academic debates.

---

[122] Howard Gardner, *Five Minds for the Future*, (Cambridge, MA: Harvard Business Review Press, 2009).

[123] R. J. Sternberg, *Wisdom, Intelligence, and Creativity Synthesized* (New York: Cambridge University Press, 2003).

[124] E. Morin, "Seven Complex Lessons in Education for the Future," UNESCO (1999).

[125] Along the way, it was found that the distinction of moral behavior versus performance is difficult and partially duplicative. The distinction between inter- and intrapersonal is also unnecessary for the same reasons.

| Essential Qualities | Associated Qualities and Concepts (non-exhaustive) |
|---|---|
| **Mindfulness** | Self-awareness, self-actualization, observation, reflection, consciousness, compassion, gratitude, empathy, growth, vision, insight, equanimity, happiness, presence, authenticity, listening, sharing, interconnectedness, interdependence, oneness, acceptance, beauty, sensibility, patience, tranquility, balance, spirituality, existentiality, social awareness, cross-cultural awareness, etc. |
| **Curiosity** | Open-mindedness, exploration, passion, self-direction, motivation, initiative, innovation, enthusiasm, wonder, appreciation, spontaneity, etc. |
| **Courage** | Bravery, determination, fortitude, confidence, risk taking, persistence, toughness, zest, optimism, inspiration, energy, vigor, zeal, cheerfulness, humor, etc. |
| **Resilience** | Perseverance, grit, tenacity, resourcefulness, spunk, self-discipline, effort, diligence, commitment, self-control, self-esteem, confidence, stability, adaptability, dealing with ambiguity, flexibility, feedback, etc. |
| **Ethics** | Benevolence, humaneness, integrity, respect, justice, equity, fairness, compassion, kindness, altruism, inclusiveness, tolerance, acceptance, loyalty, honesty, truthfulness, authenticity, genuineness, trustworthiness, decency, consideration, forgiveness, virtue, love, care, helpfulness, generosity, charity, devotion, belonging, etc. |
| **Leadership** | Responsibility, abnegation, accountability, dependability, reliability, conscientiousness, selflessness, humbleness, modesty, self-reflection, inspiration, organization, delegation, mentorship, commitment, heroism, charisma, followership, engagement, leading by example, goal-orientation, focus, results orientation, precision, execution, efficiency, negotiation, consistency, socialization, diversity, decorum, etc. |

Table 5.2 Essential Qualities of Character
*Source:* CCR

In the following sections, we will describe the relevant research literature for the six character qualities. See Chapter 7, "Briefly Touching on the *How*," for a brief discussion of how each of these character qualities can be taught.

# Mindfulness

Self-awareness, self-esteem, self-actualization, growth, vision, insight, observation, consciousness, compassion, listening, presence, sharing, interconnectedness, empathy, sensibility, patience, acceptance, appreciation, tranquility, balance, spirituality, existentiality, oneness, beauty, gratitude, interdependency, happiness, etc.

If every 8 year old in the world is taught meditation, we will eliminate violence from the world within one generation.

—Dalai Lama

The practice of mindfulness comes from Eastern spiritual philosophy. It was first translated from Sanskrit into English by British scholars in 1784, and had a strong influence on a wide range of Western thinkers. In America after World War II, Zen Buddhism, in particular, experienced a boom in interest and practice both in the intellectual and public spheres.[126] In addition to fulfilling a spiritual role, mindfulness has been used successfully for clinical purposes (treating stress, chronic pain, anxiety, depression, borderline personality disorder, eating disorders, and addiction), and is increasingly being adopted by educators as a practice that helps students reduce stress, increases their focused attention, and enhances the quality of students' everyday life.[127]

Mindfulness can be defined as "the awareness that emerges through paying attention on purpose, in the present moment and non-judgmentally, to the unfolding of experiences moment by moment."[128] Although it is common to practice mindfulness

---

[126] D. McCown, D. Reibel, and Marc S. Micozzi, *Teaching Mindfulness: A Practical Guide for Clinicians and Educators* (New York: Springer, 2010).
[127] K.E. Hooker and I. E. Fodor "Teaching Mindfulness to Children," *Gestalt Review* 12, no. 1 (2008): 75–91.
[128] J. Kabat-Zinn, *Full Catastrophe Living: Using the Wisdom of Your Body and Mind to Face Stress, Pain, and Illness* (New York: Delacorte, 1990).

through meditation techniques, the two should not be seen as the same thing, as mindfulness can be practiced through any daily experience such as eating, walking, driving, and so on.

Ellen Langer famously argues that the traditional view of no pain, no gain education—in which learning occurs with repetitive drills, constant studying, and long bouts of unwavering focus—is designed for a perfectly static, predictable environment. That for the constantly changing environment we now live in, mindfulness education is far more relevant and effective.[129] Research suggests that mindfulness training can enhance attention and focus, and improve memory, self-acceptance, self-management skills, and self-understanding,[130] although the size of the effect is often debated. It has also been associated with "higher positive emotional affect, vitality, life satisfaction, self-esteem, optimism, and self-actualization," as well as with "higher autonomy, competence, and relatedness."[131] It has also been proposed as a mechanism to address oppression[132] and a way to combat global crises, and the inability to respond to these overwhelming issues due to a lack of easy ways to translate knowledge into personal and collective action.[133] Even brief mindfulness meditation trainings have been shown to reduce fatigue and anxiety, and improve visual-spatial processing, working memory, and executive functioning.[134]

---

[129]  E. J. Langer, "A Mindful Education," *Educational Psychologist* 28, no. 1 (1993): 43–50.

[130] I.E. Fodor, and K. E. Hooker. "Teaching Mindfulness to Children," *Gestalt Review* 12, no. 1 (2008): 75–91.

[131]  K. W. Brown and R. M. Ryan, "The Benefits Of Being Present: Mindfulness And Its Role In Psychological Well-Being," *Journal of Personality and Social Psychology* 84, no. 4 (2003); 822–848.

[132]  D. Orr, "The Uses Of Mindfulness In Anti-Oppressive Pedagogies: Philosophy And Praxis," *Canadian Journal of Education* 27, no. 4 (2014): 477–497.

[133]  H. Bai, ("Beyond Educated Mind: Towards a Pedagogy of Mindfulness," in *Unfolding Bodymind: Exploring Possibilities Through Education*, eds. B. Hockings, J. Haskell, and W. Linds (Brandon, VT: The Foundation for Educational Renewal, 2001), 86–99.

[134]  F. Zeidan et al., "Mindfulness Meditation Improves Cognition: Evidence Of Brief Mental Training," *Consciousness and Cognition.* (2010)

# Curiosity

Open-mindedness, exploration, passion, self-direction, motivation, initiative, innovation, enthusiasm, spontaneity, etc.

> **I have no special talents. I am only passionately curious.**
>
> —Albert Einstein

Early discussions of curiosity as a character quality date back to Cicero, who described it as "an innate love of learning and of knowledge, without the lure of any profit,"[135] and Aristotle, who saw it as an intrinsic desire for information.[136] Modern psychology research has taken several different approaches to studying curiosity, including examining its source, situational determinants, important correlates, and relationships to motivation.

Research suggests that curiosity is both a trait (general capacity) and a state (sensitive to context and malleable with experience). It is also both an internal (homeostatic) drive as well as a response to external cues (stimulus evoked).[137] Curiosity can be conceived of as a drive (comparable to thirst or hunger) stemming from an individual's need to minimize the unpleasantness of uncertainty. Behavioral studies of organisms ranging from cockroaches to monkeys to humans have found that when deprived of sensory input they will seek out information, and that the thirst for knowledge can be satisfied with information, just as physiological thirst can be satisfied with water.

It has also been described as a response to violated expectations (or a perceptual or conceptual conflict),[138] following

---

[135] Cicero, *De Finibus Bonorum et Malorum*, H. Rackham, trans. (Cambridge, MA: Harvard Press, 1914).

[136] Aristotle, *Metaphysics* (Cambridge, MA: Harvard University Press, 1933).

[137] G. Lowenstein, "The Psychology of Curiosity: A Review and Reinterpretation," *Psychological Bulletin* 11, no. 1 (1994): 75–98.

[138] D. E. Berlyne, *Conflict, Arousal and Curiosity* (New York: McGraw-Hill, 1960).

an inverted U-shaped curve where the greatest amount of curiosity is elicited when we know enough to be interested, are surprised by what we experience, but are still uncertain of how best to make sense of the situation.[139] The optimal arousal model was arrived at separately by three different researchers in different fields: Hebb (who studied neuroscience), Piaget (who studied developmental psychology), and Hunt (who studied motivation). Curiosity has also been placed in a larger model of motivation, focusing on the drive to resolve uncertainty.[140]

This model is both intuitive and supported by research: we naturally try to understand the world around us, and this manifests as curiosity. It is highly specific to the interplay of a person's capabilities and the difficulty of the task at hand.[141] This relates to well-known psychological constructs such as cognitive dissonance, ambiguity aversion, and principles of Gestalt psychology.

The information-gap theory[142] building on these findings, models, connections, and observations, treats curiosity as the feeling resulting from paying attention to a gap in knowledge between what one knows and what one wants to know. The interest/deprivation theory combines the ideas from curiosity models with the neuroscience of desire and reward, and claims that both induction of a positive sensation of interest and reduction of the negative sensation of uncertainty are involved in curiosity.

A recent fMRI study[143] successfully found that the greater the curiosity, the more resources (time or tokens) participants were willing to spend on receiving the answer, and in line with other

---

[139]  Lowenstein, "The Psychology of Curiosity: A Review and Reinterpretation," 75-98
[140]  J. Kagan, "Motives and Development," *Journal Of Personality And Social Psychology* 22, no. 1 (1972): 51
[141]  N. Miyake and D. A. Norman, "To Ask A Question, One Must Know Enough To Know What Is Not Known," *Journal of Verbal Learning and Verbal Behavior* 18, no. 3 (1979): 357–364.
[142]  Lowenstein, "The Psychology of Curiosity," 75–98.
[143]  K.M. Jeong et al., "The Wick in the Candle of Learning Epistemic Curiosity Activates Reward Circuitry and Enhances Memory." *Psychological Science* 20, no. 8 (2009): 963–973.

mounting evidence, the more likely they were to remember the information later. Additionally, higher curiosity correlated with higher activation of areas of the brain associated with anticipated reward, prediction error, and memory.

## Courage

Bravery, determination, fortitude, confidence, risk taking, persistence, toughness, zest, optimism, inspiration, energy, vigor, zeal, cheerfulness, humor, stability, etc.

> Nothing in the world is worth having or worth doing unless it means effort, pain, difficulty... I have never in my life envied a human being who led an easy life. I have envied a great many people who led difficult lives and led them well.
>
> —Theodore Roosevelt

Courage can be thought of as the ability to act despite fear or uncertainty, in risky situations, or when we are feeling vulnerable.[144] While courage can be taken to extremes, with potentially devastating consequences, it is still true that a healthy dose of courage can be quite helpful in one's professional, social, and personal lives.

A commonly cited professional example is entrepreneurship. While studies have not found entrepreneurs to be significantly more risk-taking on self-rated measures, they have found they are courageous:

> ... multivariate tests revealed that entrepreneurs categorized equivocal business scenarios significantly more

---

[144] Brené Brown, *Daring Greatly: How the Courage to be Vulnerable Transforms The Way We Live, Love, Parent, and Lead* (New York: Penguin, 2012).

positively than did other subjects, and
univariate tests demonstrated that these
perceptual differences were consistent and
significant—that is, entrepreneurs perceived
more strengths as compared to weaknesses,
opportunities as compared to threats, and
potential for performance improvement as
compared to deterioration in the business
scenarios.[145]

In fact, one paper describes organizational failures as the consequences of "failures of courage," since none of the people responsible acted to prevent it.[146]

It is well established that risk-taking is higher in adolescents than in children or adults,[147] and higher in males than in females.[148] It is also clear that the capacity for courage is not fixed, and can be developed through appropriate learning experiences.

Courage can be considered a subjective experience, where an individual overcomes fear and chooses to take action in the face of uncertainty. In the courageous mindset there are three positive intrapersonal traits that one must develop in order to "loosen the hold that a negative emotion has gained on that person's mind and body by dismantling or undoing preparation for specific action."[149]

---

[145]   L. E. Palich and D. Ray Bagby, "Using Cognitive Theory To Explain Entrepreneurial Risk-Taking: Challenging Conventional Wisdom," *Journal of Business Venturing* 10, no. 6 (1995): 425–438, doi:10.1016/0883-9026(95)00082-J

[146]   C. R. Rate and R.J. Sternberg, "When Good People Do Nothing: A Failure Of Courage," *Research Companion to the Dysfunctional Workplac.* (Edward Elgar Publishing Limited, 2007): 3–21

[147]   L. Steinberg, "Risk Taking in Adolescence: New Perspectives From Brain and Behavioral Science," *Current Directions in Psychological Science* 16, no. 2, (2007): 55–59.

[148]   J. P. Byrnes, D. C. Miller, and W. D. Schafer, "Gender Differences in Risk Taking: A Meta-Analysis," 125 no. 3 (1999): 367–383.

[149]   B.L. Fredrickson, "The Role Of Positive Emotions In Positive Psychology: The Broaden-And-Build Theory Of Positive Emotions," *American Psychologist* 56 (2001): 218–226.

These traits are openness to experience, conscientiousness, and self-evaluation strategies that promote self-efficacy.[150]

# Resilience

Perseverance, resourcefulness, tenacity, grit, spunk, charisma, confidence, adaptability, dealing with ambiguity, flexibility, self-discipline, commitment, self-control, feedback, effort, diligence, etc.

> The greatest glory in living lies not in never falling, but in rising every time we fall.
> —Nelson Mandela

In its most basic form, resilience can be thought of as an ability or set of qualities that allow one to overcome obstacles. Resilience is the essence of the rags-to-riches stories that have permeated cultures for centuries. It often refers to the abilities of certain individuals to succeed where others in their circumstances could not. In a paper about the history of resilience and the continuing discussion on its nature, resilience is defined as "a dynamic process encompassing positive adaptation within the context of significant adversity."[151] The designation "dynamic process" highlights the fact that resilience is a word used for a multitude of factors that all influence whether or not someone will succeed in the face of adversity.

One of the contributing elements of resilience is the notion of grit. In her seminal study regarding grit—defined as "perseverance and passion for long-term goals"—Angela

---

[150] S. T. Hannah, P. J. Sweeney, and P. B. Lester, "Toward A Courageous Mindset: The Subjective Act And Experience Of Courage," *The Journal of Positive Psychology* 2, no. 2 (2007): 129–135.
[151] S. S. Luthar, D. Cicchetti, and B. Becker, "The Construct of Resilience: A Critical Evaluation and Guidelines for Future Work," Child Development 71 (2000): 543–562.

Duckworth and her colleagues found that "grit accounted for an average of 4% of the variance in success outcomes."[152]

The three main factors[153] that have been identified in schools, communities, and social support systems as positively influencing resilience in youth are:

1. Caring relationships.

2. Communication of high expectations.

3. Opportunities for meaningful involvement and participation.

As resilience is primarily concerned with overcoming adverse conditions when others might not,[154] much of the early research on resilience focuses on sample groups from high-risk communities and school systems. This research did much to identify resilience as a key factor in whether a student was likely to succeed in a high-risk setting. The identification of resilience as a positive quality led many to question the validity of certain at-risk models for reform.[155,156] Now researchers are looking at ways to encourage the positive factors that have been identified to foster resilience instead of focusing exclusively on mitigating risk factors. This has led the way for research on resilience as it relates to all students, not just those identified as high risk.[157]

---

[152] A. Duckworth et al., "Grit: Perseverance and Passion for Long-Term Goals," *Journal of Personality and Social Psychology* 92, no. 6 (2007): 1087–1101.

[153] B. Benard, "Fostering Resilience in Children," ERIC Digest (1995).

[154] P. Rees and K. Bailey, "Positive Exceptions: Learning from Students who 'Beat the Odds,'" *Educational and Child Psychology* 20, no. 4 (2003): 41–59.

[155] N. Garmezy and M. Rutter, *Stress, Coping and Development in Children* (New York: McGraw-Hill, 1983).

[156] E. Werner, "Protective Factors and Individual Resilience," in S.J.S. Meisels. ed., *Handbook of Early Childhood Intervention* (Cambridge, UK: Cambridge University Press, 1990).

[157] C. Cefai, *Promoting Resilience in the Classroom: A Guide to Developing Pupils' Emotional and Cognitive Skills* (London: Jessica Kingsley Publishers, 2008).

# Ethics

Humaneness, kindness, respect, justice, equity, fairness, compassion, tolerance, inclusiveness, integrity, loyalty, honesty, truthfulness, trustworthiness, decency, authenticity, genuineness, consideration, forgiveness, virtue, love, care, helpfulness, generosity, charity, devotion, belonging, etc.

> To educate a person in mind and not in morals is to educate a menace to society.
> —Theodore Roosevelt

Ethics as a teachable character quality is informed in large part by the literature on moral development, pioneered by Jean Piaget and John Dewey, and expanded by Lawrence Kohlberg and Carol Gilligan. The main idea is that children naturally progress through stages of moral reasoning, from pre-conventional (obedience and punishment, self-interest orientations), through conventional (interpersonal accord and conformity, authority and social-order maintaining ), to post-conventional (social contract orientation, universal ethical principles).[158]

John Dewey proposed that "education is the work of supplying the conditions which will enable the psychological functions to mature in the freest and fullest manner."[159] Environments that successfully encourage moral development are those that provide opportunities for group participation, shared decision-making, and the assumption of responsibility for the consequences of actions.[160] At the classroom level, Kohlberg proposed three conditions conducive to moral discussion:

---

[158] L. Kohlberg, *The Philosophy Of Moral Development: Moral Stages And The Idea Of Justice (Essays On Moral Development, Volume 1)* (San Francisco: Harper and Row, 1981).

[159] J. Dewey as cited in L. Kohlberg and R. H. Hersh, "Moral Development: A Review of the Theory," *Theory into Practice* 16, no. 2, (1977): 53–59.

[160] L. Kohlberg, "Moral Stages, Moralization: the Cognitive Developmental Approach," In: T. Lickona, ed. *Moral Development And Behavior* (New York: Holt, Rinehart, Winston, 1976), 54 as cited in R. M. Krawczyk, "Teaching

1. Exposure to the next higher stage of reasoning.

2. Exposure to situations posing problems and contradictions for the student's current moral structure, leading to dissatisfaction with his current level.

3. An atmosphere of interchange and dialogue combining the first two conditions, in which conflicting moral views are compared in an open manner.[161]

It is important to note that, knowledge of ethics does not necessarily lead to ethical action. Moral behavior is highly dependent on context and as such it can involve factors like motivation and emotion, or other necessary qualities like courage, as well as having strong ethical role models to follow.

A study linking moral reasoning stages and strength of will with the prevalence of cheating behavior found that 15 percent of students who were at a post-conventional stage cheated (compared to 55 percent of conventional subjects and 70 percent of pre-conventional subjects). Notably, within the conventional stage only 26 percent of what the study called strong-willed participants cheated, compared to 74 percent of those determined by the study to be weak-willed.[162] For these reasons, it is appropriate to think of ethics as a character quality rather than a knowledge domain, though studying ethical principles embedded in various subject areas (e.g., bioethics) may have some influence on ethical behavior.

---

Ethics: Effect on Moral Development," *Nursing Ethics* 4, no. 1 (January 1997): 57–65.

[161] L. Kohlberg, "The Cognitive-Developmental Approach to Moral Education," *The Phi Delta Kappan* 56, no. 10 (1975): 670–677.

[162] R. L. Krebs and L. Kohlberg, "Moral Judgment And Ego Controls As Determinants Of Resistance To Cheating," *Moral Education Research Foundation*, (1973) quoted in Kohlberg, "The Cognitive-Developmental Approach to Moral Education," 670–677.

# Leadership

Responsibility, heroism, abnegation, accountability, selflessness, humbleness, inspiration, integrity, organization, delegation, teamwork, mentorship, commitment, engagement, leading by example, goal orientation, consistency, self-reflection, social awareness, cross-cultural awareness, dependability, reliability, conscientiousness, efficiency, productivity, results orientation, focus, precision, project management, execution, socialization, negotiation, diversity, decorum, etc.

> To lead people, walk beside them... As for the best leaders, the people do not notice their existence. The next best, the people honor and praise. The next, the people fear; and the next, the people hate... When the best leader's work is done the people say, "We did it ourselves!"
>
> —Lao-Tsu

While the need for organizations to have effective leaders is undisputed, the notion of what is involved in leadership and how it can be taught is currently in the process of shifting. The traditional views can be described as falling into a systems control framework, with leaders conceived of as extraordinary, charismatic, almost superhero individuals who work in an isolated way to inspire followers to act for the good of a unitary and fixed organization. This is in line with a general mechanistic view of organizations with subordinates viewed as followers and leaders viewed as experts who attempt to maximize their control and motivate subordinates to act in certain ways to reach an organization's goals and mission.[163]

However, this view suggests that leadership is reserved for special individuals (out of reach for the majority of people) and to a great extent innate and unteachable. It is also at odds with studies

---

[163] A. Hay and M. Hodgkinson, "Rethinking Leadership: A Way Forward for Teaching Leadership?" *Leadership and Organization Development Journal* 27, no. 2 (2006): 144–158.

that have looked at the importance of quiet leadership,[164] and that successful leaders often do not fit the traditional hero description; rather they can be "shy, unpretentious, awkward and modest but at the same time [have] an enormous amount of ambition not for themselves but for the organization."[165]

The emerging process-relational framework of leadership, by contrast, emphasizes that organizations are social constructs composed of "ongoing patterns of meaning-making and activity brought about as... people [are] in relationships with each other and to their cultures."[166] In this view, leadership is not about any one individual, but a set of processes, practices, and interactions,[167] and complete control is neither possible nor desirable. Leaders, just like everyone else, must constantly make sense of crosscutting and often conflicting goals and information, and the skills they need (such as negotiation and asking insightful questions) are both more learnable and more practical.[168] This framework also allows for a greater degree of flexibility and uncertainty, with group processes seen as more important than an individual's vision.

This framework is also in line with current complex systems science models of best practices for management, in which the individual leader facilitates group processes and relationships rather than imposing his or her vision top–down, thus limiting the organization's capacity to that of one individual.[169] This shift in

---

[164] J. L. Badaracco, "We Don't Need Another Hero," *Harvard Business Review* 79, no. 8 (2001): 121–126.

[165] J. Collins, "Level 5 Leadership: The Triumph Of Humility And Fierce Resolve" *Harvard Business Review* 79, no.1 (2001): 67–76.

[166] T.J. Watson, *Organizing and Managing Work*, Prentice Hall: London (2002): 6, quoted in A. Hay and M. Hodgkinson, "Rethinking Leadership: a way forward for teaching leadership?" *Leadership and Organization Development Journal* 27, no. 2 (2006).

[167] L. Crevani, M. Lindgren, and J. Packendorff, "Leadership, Not Leaders: On The Study Of Leadership As Practices And Interactions," *Scandinavian Journal of Management* 26, no. 1 (2010); 77–86.

[168] Hay and Hodgkinson, "Rethinking Leadership" (2006).

[169] Y. Bar-Yam, "Complexity Rising: From Human Beings To Human Civilization, A Complexity Profile," *Encyclopedia of Life Support Systems* (EOLSS UNESCO Publishers, Oxford, UK, 2002).

conceptions of leadership from lone hero to a relational, collectivist, and non-authoritarian approach allows for more detailed and thoughtful decision making and greater flexibility in responding to the increasing complexity and uncertainty of our world.

A widely accepted model of teaching leadership defines leadership as a "relational and ethical process of people attempting to accomplish positive change together."[170] This relational model of leadership includes dimensions of being inclusive, empowering, purposeful, ethical, and process oriented.

---

[170] S. R. Komives, N. Lucas, and T. R. McMahon, *Exploring Leadership: For College Students Who Want to Make a Difference,* 2nd ed. (San Francisco: Jossey-Bass/Wiley, 2006).

# Chapter Six

# The Meta-Learning Dimension

> The illiterate of the twenty-first century will not be those who cannot read and write, but those who cannot learn, unlearn, and relearn.
> —Psychologist Herbert Gerjuoy as quoted by Alvin Toffler, Futurist, in Future Shock[171]

In addition to redesigning relevant knowledge, skills, and character qualities necessary for the twenty-first century, we believe that there needs to be a meta layer of education, in which students practice reflection, learn about their learning, internalize a growth mindset that encourages them to strive, and learn how to adapt their learning and behavior based on their goals. The OECD has described this dimension as reflectiveness. The EU Reference Framework of Key Competencies, the Hewlett Foundation Deeper Learning Competencies, and the Assessment and Teaching of Twenty-First Century Skills all refer to it as "learning how to learn."

The surest way to prepare students for a changing world is to give them the tools to be versatile, reflective, self-directed and self-reliant.

---

[171] Flexnib, "That Alvin Toffler Quotation," http://www.flexnib.com/2013/07/03/that-alvin-toffler-quotation

# Metacognition—Reflecting on Learning Goals, Strategies, and Results

Metacognition, simply put, is *the process of thinking about thinking*. It is important in every aspect of school and life, since it involves self-reflection on one's current position, future goals, potential actions and strategies, and results. At its core, it is a basic survival strategy, and has been shown to be present even in rats.[172]

Perhaps the most important reason for developing metacognition is that it can improve the application of knowledge, skills, and character qualities in realms beyond the immediate context in which they were learned.[173] This can result in the transfer of competencies across disciplines—important for students preparing for real-life situations where clear-cut divisions of disciplines fall away and one must select competencies from the entire gamut of their experience to effectively apply them to the challenges at hand. Even within academic settings, it is valuable—and often necessary—to apply principles and methods across disciplinary lines. Transfer can also be necessary within a discipline, such as when a particular idea or skill was learned with one example, but students must know how to apply it to another task to complete their homework or exams, or to a different context. Transfer is the ultimate goal of all education, as students are expected to internalize what they learn in school and apply it to life.

---

[172] Rats were presented with a task that they could choose to decline; they received a higher reward if they declined than if they failed the task. As expected, the frequency of declining increased with the difficulty of the task, and accuracy was higher on trials where the rats chose to complete the task compared with trials when they were forced to. See A. L. Foote and J. D. Crystal, "Metacognition in the Rat," *Current Biology* 17, no. 6 (2007): 551–555.
[173] Gregory Schraw and David Moshman, "Metacognitive Theories," *Educational Psychology Papers and Publications*, Paper 40 (1995).

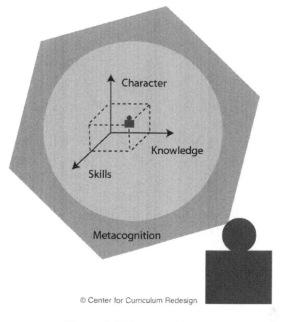

Figure 6.1 Metacognition
*Source:* CCR

To illustrate the value of metacognition and how it actually plays a role in learning, we can consider an example from mathematics, where it has been shown that metacognition plays a central role in learning and achievement.[174] Specifically, when novice students were compared to seasoned mathematicians, the students selected a seemingly useful strategy and continued to apply it without checking to see if the strategy of choice was actually working well. Thus, a significant amount of time was wasted in fruitless pursuits. The more experienced mathematicians on the other hand, exercised metacognition, monitoring their approach all along the way to see if it was actually leading to a solution or merely to a dead end.[175] Being aware of how one is engaging with the process of learning influences how the student interprets the task at hand, and what strategies are selected and

[174] Z. Mevarech, and B. Kramarski, *Critical Maths for Innovative Societies: The Role of Metacognitive Pedagogies* (Paris, France: OECD Publishing, 2014).
[175] A. Gourgey, "Metacognition in Basic Skills Instruction," *Instructional Science* 26, no. 1 (1998): 81–96.

employed in service of achieving learning goals. It can help optimize the problem-solving experience at a very high level, and is thus applicable across a large range of contexts. These metacognitive strategies are powerful tools for any discipline, inter-discipline or for learning in general.

Of course, with such an abstract learning goal, it is important for educators to be precise with how they teach it. Traditional methods for improving students' learning strategies often focus on prescribed procedures (note-taking, self-testing, scheduling, etc.) and typically result in initial motivation and some short-term improvement, but ultimately a reversion to old habits happens.[176] While these tactics may work in the short term (e.g., to cram for an exam), once the context changes, successful transfer of these methods is less likely to occur. More strategic methods that focus on metacognition for deeper learning—such as developing a growth mindset (discussed later), setting and monitoring one's learning goals, and growing one's capacity to persist despite difficulties—have been shown to result in more permanent learning gains.[177]

It is important to note that since metacognition involves higher-level thinking overseeing lower-level thoughts, there is actually a range of mental processes that fall under its definition. Effects of metacognitive training vary based on *what* kind of lower-level thoughts are being overseen, and *how* they are being overseen. Research has identified three levels of reporting on metacognitive processes:

> 1. Verbalization of knowledge that is already in a verbal state (such as recalling what happened in a story).

---

[176] E. Martin and P. Ramsden, "Learning Skills and Skill in Learning," in J.T.E. Richardson, M. Eysenck, and D. Warren-Piper (Eds.), *Student Learning: Research in Education and Cognitive Psychology* (Guildford, Surrey: Society for Research into Higher Education and NFER-Nelson, 1986) as cited in J. Biggs, "The Role of Metacognition in Enhancing Learning," *Australian Journal of Education* 32, no. 2, (1988): 127–138.
[177] Biggs, "The Role of Metacognition in Enhancing Learning," 127–138.

2. Verbalization of nonverbal knowledge (such as recalling how one solved a Rubik's Cube).

3. Verbalization of *explanations* of verbal or nonverbal knowledge (such as explaining how one makes use of the rhetorical structures of a story as one reads).

Only this third level of metacognitive process has been linked to improved results in problem solving.[178]

Metacognition can be developed in students in the context of their current goals and can enhance their learning of competencies[179] as well as transfer of learning,[180] no matter their starting achievement level. In fact, it may be most useful for lower-achieving students, as the higher-achieving students are already employing strategies that have proven successful for them.[181] For learning disabled and low-achieving students, metacognitive training has been shown to improve behavior more effectively than traditional attention-control training.[182]

Students who have higher levels of self-efficacy (more confidence in their ability to achieve their goals) are more likely to engage in metacognition and, in turn, are more likely to perform at

---

[178] D. J. Hacker and J. Dunlosky, "Not All Metacognition Is Created Equal," *New Directions for Teaching and Learning* 95 (2003): 73–79.

[179] A. M. Schmidt and J. K. Ford, "Learning Within a Learner Control Training Environment: the Interactive Effects of Goal Orientation and Metacognitive Instruction on Learning Outcomes," *Personnel Psychology* 56, no. 2 (2003): 405–429.

[180] J. K. Ford et al., "Relationships of Goal Orientation, Metacognitive Activity, and Practice Strategies With Learning Outcomes and Transfer," *Journal of Applied Psychology* 83, no. 2 (1998): 218–233.

[181] W. J. McKeachie, "The Need for Study Strategy Training," In C. E. Weinstein, E. T. Goetz, and P. A. Alexander, eds., *Learning And Study Strategies: Issues In Assessment, Instruction, And Evaluation* (New York: Academic Press, 1988), 3–9.

[182] K. A. Larson and M. M. Gerber, "Effects of Social Metacognitive Training of Enhanced Overt Behavior in Learning Disabled and Low Achieving Delinquents," *Exceptional Children* 54, no.3 (1987), 201–211

higher levels.[183] This strongly indicates a positive feedback loop for high-achieving students—they are more successful by using metacognitive strategies, which increases their confidence and in turn leads them to continue to increase their performance. Metacognition is an integral part of this virtuous learning cycle, and one that is amenable to further improvement through instruction.

# Internalizing a Growth Mindset

Without having to think about it, students have all absorbed from society some mix of messages about themselves, their talents, and the importance of hard work. We see this underlying model expressed in many different ways. Students often brag about how little they studied for a particular exam that they did well on, or claim to be "just not good at" one subject or another. These and a plethora of other student behaviors are clues into their subconscious models for how much talent and hard work contribute to success.

According to Carol Dweck's research, there are two broad categories of these mental models for success. In a fixed mindset, people believe their basic qualities, like their intelligence or talent, are simply fixed traits. They spend their time documenting their intelligence or talent instead of developing them. They also believe that talent alone creates success—without effort. This leads to self-defeating patterns of behavior that the students aren't even aware they are engaging in. In a growth mindset, on the other hand, people recognize that talent is just the starting point, and believe that abilities can be developed through hard work. This view creates a love of learning for the sake of learning, and a resilience that is essential for success in large endeavors.

---

[183] Kanfer and Ackerman, 1989 and Bouffard-Bouchard, Parent, and Larivee, 1991, as cited in S. Coutinho, "Self-Efficacy, Metacognition, and Performance," *North American Journal of Psychology* 10, no. 1 (2008): 165–172.

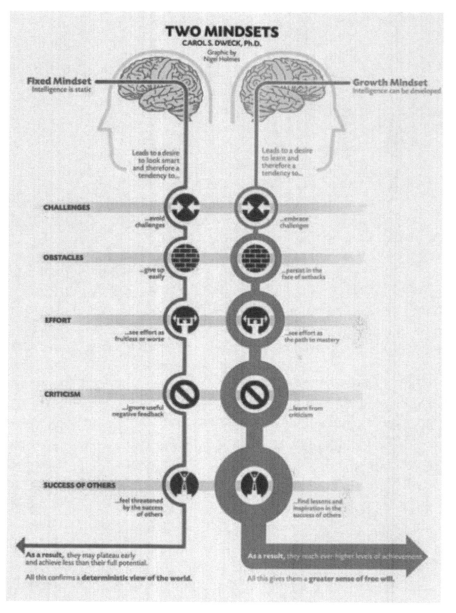

Figure 6.2 Two Mindsets
*Source: Mindset* by Carol Dweck

Of course, *both* natural talent and hard work contribute to success. Alfred Binet, the inventor of the IQ test, believed that education was crucial to increasing our intelligence:

Some recent philosophers seem to have given their moral approval to these deplorable verdicts that affirm that the intelligence of an individual is a fixed quantity, a quantity that cannot be augmented. We must protest and react against this brutal pessimism; we will try to demonstrate that it is founded on nothing… With practice, training, and above all, method, we manage to increase our attention, our memory, our judgment and literally to become more intelligent than we were before.[184]

We are now learning more about how people are able to increase, through practice, capacities that seemed fixed. Herbert Nitsch, a world champion free diver,[185] can hold his breath for over nine minutes. We used to think the brain did not change; we then recognized the existence of certain periods of development in which the brain changed. We now know that the brain quite literally changes based on experience in every single moment, and it is the collective effects of these experiences that result in our personalities, and our conscious experiences.

So how does mindset affect students' interactions with their goals in school?

Students who have a learning goal (associated with a growth mindset) are concerned with internalizing the skills, understandings, and mindsets of the lesson. Students with a performance goal (associated with a fixed mindset) are mostly concerned with being perceived as having mastered what is being taught. Learning-oriented students tend to see mistakes as opportunities for growth and improvement, while performance-

---

[184] Baldwin Hergenhahn and Tracy Henley. *An Introduction to the History of Psychology*, 7th ed. (Belmont, CA: Cengage Learning, 2013).

[185] Free diving is the practice of diving without the use of any external breathing apparatus.

oriented students see them as failures. As a result, learning-oriented students expend more effort when confronted with challenges, whereas performance-oriented students expend less.[186]

Students with a learning orientation tend to employ more metacognitive strategies and attain higher levels of academic achievement.[187] These internal views of personal learning capacity implicitly and explicitly influence students' metacognitive processes as early as third grade[188] and learning strategies are employed, (or not!), accordingly.

# The Importance of Meta-Learning

As adults, we no longer get all of our goals and deadlines decided and enforced for us. The majority of most people's lives will be spent out of school, and will require internal motivation to continue to grow and develop in order to live fulfilling lives and meet the challenges facing society. The more we learn, the more our previous conceptions of the world get outdated. In clinical research for example, the half-life of truth is 45 years.[189] This means that half of what doctors learned in school, if they don't update their knowledge themselves, is wrong by the time they retire. There is reason to believe that even people who decide they want to keep learning struggle to do so. On average, only 7 percent of people who sign up for an online class follow it through to

---

[186] D. B. Miele, L. K. Son, and J. Metcalfe, "Children's Naive Theories of Intelligence Influence Their Metacognitive Judgments," *Child Development* 84, no. 6 (2013): 1879–1886.

[187] S. A. Coutinho, "The Relationship Between Goals, Metacognition, and Academic Success," *Educate* 7, no. 1 (2007): 39–47.

[188] Miele, Son, and Metcalfe, "Children's Naive Theories," 1879–1886.

[189] T. Poynard et al., "Truth Survival in Clinical Research: An Evidence-Based Requiem?" *Annals of Internal Medicine* 136, no. 12 (2002): 888–895.

completion.[190] We need meta-learning to be able to effectively recognize our weaknesses and push ourselves to improve.

Education without meta-learning is only so effective, as there is evidence that people do not apply their understanding— even if they have deep understanding!—to their decisions in the world. In one study, researchers examined whether ethicists were more ethical in their lives:

> The evidence suggests that they are no
> likelier to donate to charity, to choose a
> vegetarian diet, to reply to student emails, to
> pay conference registration fees they owe, to
> return their library books, to vote in public
> elections, to stay in regular contact with
> their mothers, to be blood or organ donors,
> or to behave politely at conferences.[191]

So metacognition is key to recognizing opportunities for improvement and a growth mindset is necessary to believe that one can successfully improve. After that, metacognition is needed to effectively plan, monitor, and evaluate one's learning strategies.

Meta-learning is the fourth dimension of education that can help all students with the varied tasks of learning in the present and the future, as well as all of the jobs and personal choices individuals must make during their lifetimes. It is the internalized voice that says, "Okay, how do I know that this is the right thing to do?" and the voice that says "I can do this, if I keep trying." It supports and rounds out every other dimension of education (knowledge, skills, and character), by creating goals and feedback loops in which students continue to improve and thrive, without teachers or parents prodding them at every step. It sets students up to succeed in lifelong, self-directed learning, in the productive

---

[190] Chris Parr, "Not Staying the Course," *Inside Higher Ed,*
www.insidehighered.com/news/2013/05/10/new-study-low-mooc-completion-rates
[191] E. Schwitzgebel, "The Moral Behavior of Ethicists and the Role of the Philosopher" in *Experimental Ethics: Toward an Empirical Moral Philosophy,* C. Luetge, H. Rusch, and M. Uhl, eds. (New York: MacMillan, 2013).

careers they may choose, and in continuing to grow throughout their lives, as the world continues to shift what is needed to be an effective, well-rounded twenty-first century person.

# Chapter Seven

# Briefly Touching on the *How*

## A Feedback Loop between *What* and *How*

Although this book is all about the *what* of education, we understand the importance of the feedback loop between the *what* and the *how*. Jurisdictions generally decide what standards and assessments get implemented, allowing for some flexibility (or not) in local, school-level decisions. And schools, in return, provide feedback from the practices of curriculum and instruction and what works or not, as measured by assessments, evaluations, and research and development (R&D).

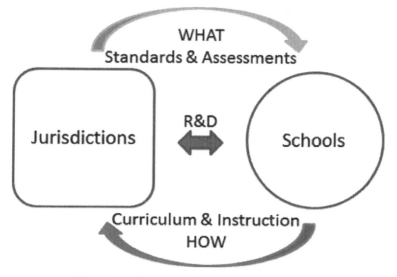

Figure 7.1 *What* and *How* Feedback Loop
Source: CCR

We also understand the importance of the *how* to students and teachers in the classroom. The same topic, covered in one way will be uninteresting and ineffective, but covered another way can have practical, cognitive, and emotional value that lasts a lifetime.

From the sections on skills, character, and meta-learning, it seems implausible that, for instance, courage could be developed strictly through classroom time, or that communication could be developed through passive listening of a lecture. The *if-done-well* caveat mentioned earlier hinges on practices that match the content and education goals. Practices to shape twenty-first century learners include learning activities to build knowledge, learn skills, develop character qualities, and apply meta-learning strategies. These activities often go beyond didactic lecturing, into project-based learning, inquiry learning, debate, design, performance, expedition, sport, contemplation, and play. Of course, the appropriate use of technology in the classroom also matters. Here we will just briefly address this important issue.

# The Interplay with Technology

[Note: this section is not about describing all the possible uses of education technology, nor proposing a proof of its efficacy—this would require an entire other book. The only goal here is to quickly highlight the potential of such endeavors.]

We often hear people ask: how can we use technology in the classroom? But a better question would be, how can technology *enhance* what we aim to do in the classroom? Teaching is the priority; the technology ought to be invisible. If we showcase technology in our schools, we are missing the point; we ought to showcase the learning that the technology enables. Content and competence must be king and queen.[192]

---

[192]   P. Nilsson, "The Challenge of Innovation," *Critical Thinking and Creativity: Learning Outside the Box Conference*. Bilkent University (2011).

When we consider all the ways technology can help education, it is important to remember that it is neither a silver bullet, nor is it going to ruin education. Technology is not an end in itself; it is a set of useful tools to enhance students' educational experiences and learning.

If a student is not in the habit of sense-making while doing math problems, for instance, a computer will only hide and exacerbate this missing skill. The student may be able to just get by with a superficial understanding of the concept, using technology to help cover up this lack of deep understanding. There is also technology to help overcome this same problem. For example, using the QAMA calculator,[193] students must enter an appropriate estimate before they are shown the correct answer.[194] So, technology can be a tool that promotes more superficial understanding, but it can also be a tool to develop deeper understanding.

A strength of technology is that it has processing power that students can learn to use to their advantage, crunching many more logic algorithms and data than they could by hand. In doing so, technology frees the space and time for students to practice and improve higher level thinking skills. For instance, software can be used as a tool for solving complex math problems involving real-world data and programming. This is the critical difference between computer-assisted and computer-based[195] mathematics education—computer-assisted education does not use the technology to enhance learning, but rather simply transposes traditional learning to a computer interface. Computer-based learning, on the other hand, uses computers as tools that students use to train their higher level thinking skills.

Another benefit of technology is that it exposes students to an incredible amount of global resources and diverse ideas. Students must learn to be critical consumers of information in a

---

[193] QAMA, http://qamacalculator.com

[194] How close is close enough is the special sauce of the algorithms in the calculator.

[195] Computer-based math, www.computerbasedmath.org

world where every possible opinion is expressed—What does it mean that this blogger interpreted this study one way, and this other one interpreted it a different way? What does it mean when one study found something to be true, and another study found it to be false? Students need to learn good rules of thumb for dealing with an information-rich and opinion-rife environment (this is the goal of the information literacy theme described earlier).

Technology also has the capacity to connect students to people from all over the world. In the not too distant past, pen-pal activities took a lot of logistical planning and were limited to sending letters back and forth with a long delay; we now have the capacity to connect instantly with people who share similar interests, with those we disagree with, and those who are different from us. This provides us with wonderful opportunities to learn about other cultures, our own selves, and to practice the communication, collaboration, and critical and creative thinking skills necessary to live in an interconnected world.

Finally, technology has the capacity to be personalized for each student according to his or her needs, though it will take time for this potential to be fully realized. In the future, technology can adapt and learn from a student's actions, and from the latest research, learning theories and potential pathways for personalized learning, and present to students optimum amounts of feedback, the appropriate level of difficulty for learning challenges, and also signal to the teacher the needed guidance that would be most helpful. Learning can be as immersive and exciting as video games and virtual-reality environments, where student autonomy, the goal of mastery, and a larger purpose are motivations for learning. Progress can be tracked by assessments fully integrated with learning, formatively guiding student experiences, incorporating in real time the shifts in instruction as needed, and continuously tuning the learning progressions.

# Chapter Eight

# Concluding Thoughts

## Education, Evidence, and Action

Some may argue that there is not yet enough scientific evidence to conclude that all of the dimensions and elements of the framework presented in this book would truly benefit humanity if they were taught well. After all, science has not yet proven beyond a reasonable doubt that they would.

There is a danger in believing in a false dichotomy about scientific fact—either science has 100 percent proven something to be true, or we are unable to say anything about it at this time. Even well-established scientific concepts such as evolution are currently suffering from this kind of false critique, with some people believing that since it hasn't been "totally proven" it may as well have been proven false.

We believe that all of us have a responsibility to do the best we can in the design of education, even in the face of uncertainty. One of the reasons for the incompleteness of evidence is that these expanded educational goals and measures of social progress are more difficult to evaluate than memorized content or very basic skills like arithmetic. Yet we believe that the curriculum should not be determined by how easy or difficult various outcomes are to measure. We want to avoid the streetlight effect, or observational bias—only looking for answers where we expect we can find them.[196] We therefore have purposely come from a practical notion of world needs and appropriate educational goals, synthesizing a framework for the education we need, not an incremental increase on the education we have.

In reality, scientists are constantly swimming in pools of shallower and deeper uncertainty. And decision makers must frequently act without 100% proof. The real world rarely operates on absolutes. We must remember that not acting to change the current education system is itself an action, and one that we have strong evidence to believe will only perpetuate existing problems. The current system is not succeeding in the ambitious goal of preparing all students for success in the twenty-first century, and the gaps between what students need and what they are receiving in schools have not been closing fast enough. Failing to improve the system because of a false standard of absolute scientific proof is not a viable option.

The current education systems should also not receive a free pass on proof. When examined critically, there is a lot of research showing the shortcomings of existing educational systems. Even for students who were successful within the current system, it is not clear that if they had they gone through a different system they wouldn't have flourished even more.

Conrad Wolfram makes the distinction between innovation-led evidence (in which a product is first built and then tested for its worthiness) and evidence-led innovation (in which formal evidence from previous products becomes the design goals for any

---

[196] The streetlight effect is a term that comes from the following story: A policeman is walking by a bar one night, and he sees a drunk man crawling around on the ground beneath a lamp post. "What are you looking for?" the cop asks the drunk man. "I'm looking for my house keys," the man says. "I lost them around here." "I'll help you," the cop says. Together, they begin to look around under the streetlight. But after a few minutes, neither one of them can find the keys. "Are you sure this is where you lost your keys?" the cop asks. "No, I'm not sure of that at all," the man says. "I might've lost them in the alley." "Then why aren't you looking in the alley?" the cop asks. "Well, this is where the light is," the drunk man says.

new products).[197] The former, he believes, is much more productive, though of course validity of the results must always be verified. The latter, however, he believes, by definition, excludes fundamental innovation because it restricts products to the space of what came before.

When one builds something significantly new it isn't just a matter of formally assembling evidence from the past in a predictable way. A leap is needed, or several—new insights from new perspectives. Often this comes from long bouts of observation, experience, iterations, and more mysterious flashes of insight. But wherever it comes from, it isn't entirely evidence-led.

More importantly, we do have increasing evidence from more and more schools and networks of schools that adopting these new learning goals, curriculum practices, and assessment methods does, in fact, make a big positive difference in the lives of students. The Hewlett Foundation's Deeper Learning initiative[198] shows through its research on over 500 schools that there is strong evidence that all students can be more successful when given opportunities to learn an expanded set of competencies, which are a part of the CCR framework elements. In a recent American Institute of Research Report the overwhelming evidence showed that:

> . . . students in high schools that were part of
> networks associated with the William and
> Flora Hewlett Foundation's Deeper
> Learning Community of Practice performed
> better than similar students in comparison
> schools on a range of measures. These
> included test scores, measures of
> interpersonal and intrapersonal skills, on-

---

[197] Conrad Wolfrram, www.conradwolfram.com/home/2015/5/21/role-of-evidence-in-education-innovation

[198] Hewlett Foundation's Deeper Learning Initiative, http://www.hewlett.org/programs/education/deeper-learning

time high school graduation rates, and
college enrollment rates. [199]

We can do better than our current system; we must
synthesize and learn from all of the expertise we have gained, and
then make a well-considered leap, in order to innovate.

# Societal Meta-Learning

In essence, another way of looking at what has been
presented here is that we are all collectively engaged in a large
meta-learning process with our societies. We are examining our
learning goals and strategies, constantly monitoring and reflecting
on our progress and setbacks, and continuously learning from our
experiences, trying out new innovations as we go—all to redesign
education for our times.

This book is one step in that direction. We have
summarized the challenges facing our twenty-first century world
and offered our best prescriptions for the education goals that will
best meet these challenges into the future—these are the
dimensions of our framework for twenty-first century learning.

We wish to get your feedback in the comments section of
the book's website, incorporate it into updates of this work, and
begin helping, where needed, to act on the lessons learned and to
continue to innovate. We are using a distribution model, described
in the introduction, commensurate with this evolutionary approach
to co-redesigning the curriculum.

We can think of no greater challenge or more exciting
journey than helping to redesign education goals and learning
experiences that will prepare all students for their future, and
empower them to build a better future for us all. Our hope is that

---

[199] American Institute of Research Report, "Deeper Learning," August 2015,
http://educationpolicy.air.org/publications/deeper-learning-improving-student-
outcomes-college-career-and-civic-life - sthash.N6W5vWeI.dpuf

you share our excitement and wish to join us on this adventure, that all started with a very simple question: *What should students learn for the twenty-first century?*

———————————————

# Appendix

## Terminology Rationale

What needs to be considered for a correct taxonomy? In developing its top-most taxonomy, CCR has used the following logic:

  • Is the word generally comprehensible by a non-education expert?

  • Is the word generally comprehensible by non-native English speakers?

  • Does the word mean, to the greatest extent possible, the action required?

  • Is it used at the right layer of abstraction?

By this method, CCR has zeroed in on the following words, shown in Table A1.1

| Possible Words | CCR's Choice | Logic |
|---|---|---|
| Subjects; Content; Disciplines; Knowledge; Understanding | Knowledge | • Subjects are what constitute Content.<br>• Content is a subset of Knowledge.<br>• Disciplines are branches of Knowledge.<br>• Understanding is the resulting goal, and "Understandings" is clumsy and has diverse meaning. |
| 21st Century Skills; Higher Order Thinking Skills | Skills | The word "Skills" is widely understood as "using knowledge," but is vastly overused in varied contexts, from multiplication tables to entrepreneurship. CCR uses it to describe the "4 C" skills only. |
| Character, Agency, Aptitudes, Attitudes, Attributes, Behaviors, Compass, Dispositions, Personality, Temperament, Values, Social & Emotional Skills | Character | • No single word satisfies everyone.<br>• Character is used most often in countries, particularly Asia where it is less politically charged than in the US/UK.<br>• Character is understandable. by even the non-specialist.<br>• All the other terms each have their limitations and biased understanding.<br>• "Social & Emotional skills" is too long, academic sounding, and "skills" is confusing. |
| Metacognition, Learn how to learn, Reflection, Self-directed learning | Meta-Learning | • To imply "the process by which learners become aware of and increasingly in control of habits of perception, inquiry, learning, and growth that they have internalized."<br>• Separating this into a fourth dimension, as difficult as it is, allows for extra focus rather than subsuming under skills, given the importance of this dimension.<br>• "Metacognition" is overly technical and may be confusing in other languages<br>• Meta-Learning captures the placement of this level as adding depth and effectiveness of the other three dimensions, and reflection and adaptation of one's learning methods and outcomes. |

Table A1.1 CCR Taxonomy
*Source:* CCR

# About CCR

## REDESIGNING EDUCATION STANDARDS

The Center for Curriculum Redesign (CCR) is an international convening body and research center seeking to expand humanity's potential and improve collective prosperity by redesigning K–12 education standards for the twenty-first century. In order to create a comprehensive set of frameworks, CCR brings together constituencies with diverse points of view—international organizations, jurisdictions, academic institutions, corporations, and nonprofit organizations including foundations—to consider and respond to the question: "What should students learn for the twenty-first century?"

## THE CENTER'S GUIDING PRINCIPLES

A sustainable humanity—one in which collective potential is expanded, and collective prosperity improved—is orchestrated out of multiple social, economic, and environmental factors. Key among them: a relevant education, based on meaningful curriculum, is critical to creating sustainability, balance, and wellbeing.

While significant attention is being paid to teaching methods and pedagogy, the CCR argues that the *what* of K–12 education is at least as important as the *how*, and brings a singular focus to the what.

That twenty-first century what must take into account the accelerated pace of change we are experiencing, and shifts in societal and personal needs. Curriculum must be useful for the lives children will live and adapted accordingly.

Our ability to contribute a meaningful WHAT requires openness to different perspectives. Therefore, CCR avoids dogma and emphasizes innovation and synthesis—multiple inputs applied and organized for optimum clarity and impact.

*We can—and will—shape the future we want.*

# FOCUS ON THE *WHAT*

Exponential changes in technology make specific predictions about the future all the more unreliable, but one thing is certain: we must prepare children to deal with greater complexity than ever before. The last major curriculum reform occurred in the late 1800s, also in a time of rapidly changing needs. Well into the twenty-first century, we can ill afford to depend on a nineteenth century curriculum. Indeed, we cannot expect our children to thrive unless we deeply examine, redesign and deliver a curriculum consistent with twenty-first century needs—one that is balanced and flexible. To thrive will mean to be adaptable and versatile.

In designing a curriculum framework around adaptability and versatility we accomplish two main goals:

1. Enhance the chances of an individual's personal and professional success and fulfillment.

2. Provide a common base of understanding and ability to participate in society, for a sustainable humanity.

# THE CENTER'S WORK

The Center for Curriculum Redesign is not a program or intervention. The staff and CCR's partners approach their work holistically, actively engaging with policymakers, standard setters, curriculum and assessment developers, school administrators, heads of schools, department heads, key teachers and other thought leaders and influencers to develop a thorough understanding of the needs and challenges of all education stakeholders. This is essential to creating the vision of meaningful, relevant twenty-first century education, and to enabling practical implementation.

The organization's research, findings and recommendations are actively disseminated through a wide variety of formats: CCR-sponsored conferences and seminars, active web presence and social media, consulting engagements and keynoting.

The following video links serve to summarize our views, and can be shared freely:

https://www.youtube.com/watch?v=vNGgJ3rQd9I     and https://vimeo.com/120748039

# CCR's Assessments Research Consortium

## Why an Assessment Research Consortium?

With the development of a new framework and wider goals for education, enhanced sets of measures are now needed to track progress toward those goals. In other emerging fields and industries, new standards for measurement, evaluation, and assessment of progress are often established by a pre-competitive, collaborative consortium of organizations and experts that collectively create the level playing field of research, high standards, and effective practices that will best serve all constituents.

Presently, there are numerous assessment efforts around the world that are disconnected from each other, and as a result critical mass is not reached and progress is stymied. As in other industries such as semiconductors, biotech, and many others, this consortium aims to harmonize the many disparate research efforts, and provide a critical mass behind such complex research by sharing the costs and the outputs on a pre-competitive basis.

Once the foundational research, standards, and exemplary practices are firmly in place and shared among all consortium members, it is then time to let a thousand innovative flowers bloom, both collaboratively and competitively in the global market for services and products.

The goal of an education assessment consortium is to establish a collective field for redesigned systems of measuring student, classroom, school, district, regional, state, national, and international progress in learning, aligned to 21$^{st}$ century global goals and desired education outcomes.

# How Will the Assessment Research Consortium Work?

Leaders from government, the private sector, academia, and nonprofit organizations are invited to join the consortium, which will collectively oversee key research projects to define assessments for and as learning across the CCR Framework's four dimensions of education: knowledge, skills, character, and meta-learning.

| Assessments *of* Learning | Assessments *for* Learning | Assessments *as* Learning |
|---|---|---|
| Standardized, psychometrically sound tests or tools for measuring whether students have developed knowledge, skills and other competencies compared to established standards, benchmarks and learning goals for the purpose of accountability, program evaluation, or research <br><br> * Example: *US NAEP Test* | Formative and some portfolio summative methods of identifying: student learning progress in ongoing work and performance tasks; new learning needs as they arise; and opportunities to revise work and improve competencies <br><br> * Example: *Performance Task* | Mostly formative, meaningful learning tasks with embedded assessments that provide immediate feedback as part of the ongoing learning experience, with a progression of challenges for increasing mastery with a wide variety of feedback <br><br> * Example: *Online Learning Game* |

The consortium aims to produce cutting-edge recommendations on assessments related to the framework's 12 competencies. Given the urgency of aligning education with 21$^{st}$ century societal needs, the consortium aims to complete the assessment recommendations within a three- to five-year period and advocate for rapid adoption.

CENTER for CURRICULUM REDESIGN

Making Education *More* Relevant

# About the Authors

Charles Fadel is a global education thought leader and expert, futurist, and inventor; founder and chairman of the Center for Curriculum Redesign; visiting scholar at Harvard Graduate School of Education; chair of the education committee at BIAC/OECD; co-author of best-selling book *21$^{st}$ Century Skills*; founder and president of the Fondation Helvetica Educatio (Geneva, Switzerland); senior fellow, human capital at The Conference Board; senior fellow at P21.org. He has worked with education systems and institutions in more than thirty countries. He was formerly Global Education Lead at Cisco Systems, a visiting scholar at MIT ESG and UPenn CLO, and an angel investor with Beacon Angels. He holds a BSEE, an MBA, and five patents.
Charles' full biography is at:
http://curriculumredesign.org/about/team/#charles

**Maya Bialik** is a writer, editor, and research synthesizer at CCR, who is passionate about appropriate interpretation and the application of science at the personal and the policy levels. She is also co-founder and associate director of The People's Science, a non-profit that improves the relationship between science and society. She leads workshops on science communication, improvisation, and interdisciplinarity. Maya holds a Master's degree in Mind, Brain & Education from Harvard, and her background includes research and writing in complex systems, education, environmental science, psychology, neuroscience, and linguistics. Follow her on twitter @mayabialik.

**Bernie Trilling** is founder and CEO of 21st Century Learning Advisors and the former Global Director of the Oracle Education Foundation. He has served as board member of the Partnership for 21st Century Learning (P21), co-chaired the committee that developed the P21 rainbow-learning framework, and is currently a

P21 senior fellow and an American Leadership Forum senior fellow. He was director of the Technology In Education group at WestEd, a U.S. national educational laboratory, and was executive producer for instruction at Hewlett-Packard Company, where he helped lead a pioneering global interactive distance-learning network. Bernie co-authored *21st Century Skills: Learning for Life in Our Times* and has written chapters for books such as the *Deeper Learning: Beyond 21st Century Skills* collection. He is a featured speaker and workshop leader at numerous educational gatherings.

Made in the USA
Middletown, DE
09 March 2016